CHARLIE COMPANY

By the same Author

*

Dr Johnson's Printer: the
Life of William Strahan

CHARLIE COMPANY

*In Service with C Company
2nd Queen's Own Cameron Highlanders
1940–44*

PETER COCHRANE
D.S.O., M.C.

1977
CHATTO & WINDUS
LONDON

Published by
Chatto & Windus Ltd.
40 William IV Street
London WC2N 4DF

*

Clarke, Irwin & Co. Ltd.
Toronto

British Library Cataloguing in
Publication Data

Cochrane, Peter
  Charlie Company
  1. Great Britain. Army. 2nd Queen's
Own Cameron Highlanders. C Company 2. World War, 1939–1945—
Personal narratives, British I. Title
940.54 '81 '41   D760.Q/

ISBN 0–7011–2280–3

© Peter Cochrane 1977

Printed in Great Britain by
Butler & Tanner Ltd.
Frome and London

Contents

Illustrations

Maps

AUTHOR'S NOTE

At the risk of sounding egocentric, I should perhaps explain that baptismally and hence officially my christian names are James Aikman, and so appear in all records. Since I have never been called anything but Peter, I have preferred to use that name on the title page.

FOREWORD

M Y reason for writing this book is that, by coincidence, the active service I saw in the second World
War was all with the same rifle company. It seemed worth
while to attempt to describe some of its vicissitudes. It is
not a complete story of Charlie or C Company, for I was
in hospital and then invalided home while they were
engaged in the bitter desert campaigns between June 1941
and June 1942. Nor is it in any way the story of the
2nd Battalion, The Queen's Own Cameron Highlanders,
admirably told in the regimental history (Blackwood,
1952), still less that of the 4th Indian Division.

A rifle company of course functions as part of a battalion even if detached and temporarily in an independent
role, and C Company's history would make no sense
without at least an outline of what the rest of the battalion
was doing, in the context of the brigade and divisional
plan. But a company has a strong sense of identity, and
its attention is focused primarily on its own performance,
at least in conditions of active service; hence the deliber-
ately restricted viewpoint of this narrative, and the infre-
quent mention of all my friends in the other companies
of the battalion.

It is based on a journal written up at irregular intervals
when we were out of the line and re-united with our
baggage, and also, as far as Italy is concerned, on letters
to my wife. These on re-reading prove remorselessly
cheerful, and very properly uninformative about our
serious activities, but provide some background to the
sketchy diary notes.

The grandest of global strategies in war has in the end
to be implemented by foot soldiers on their particular

little patch of ground. This account of one small group of them is dedicated to those who survived the experience, and the many who did not.

INDOCTRINATION

THE Intelligence Officer, Colin Kerr, introduced me to C Company on August 28th 1940, in the Western Desert; it was four years later in Italy that I finally said goodbye to them. Like an old knife that has had three new blades and two new handles, it was and it wasn't by then the same company. Of course the people who formed it had changed several times over, attitudes had been altered by the course of the war and by the difference between the soldier whose career was the army and the volunteer or conscript who found himself willy-nilly in a certain unit through the wild chances of military postings: and yet it still remained C Company, 2nd Battalion The Queen's Own Cameron Highlanders, and convinced that 'Wha's like us? De'il the yin.'

I had arrived at battalion headquarters the previous night by a series of trains from Port Said through the Delta and along the single track line that led to Mersa Matruh, some 200 miles west of Alexandria on the Mediterranean coast. It was difficult to see why the Egyptian State Railways had troubled to build little stations along the line, or why they had settled on one patch of waste rather than another to site them; but at Gerâwla, a hut and a name board, I got out and waited nervously and for a long time for transport to pick me up. The nervousness arose from the facts that I was a newly-commissioned wartime second lieutenant about to join a regular battalion, and that I had been posted to it from the regimental depot at Inverness four and a half months earlier. The battalion had probably long since written me off as a faulty transmission in a signal. I foresaw tedious explanations of how I had been sent back to England from Marseilles, with the troopship there in port, when the Germans irrupted into the Low Countries and Italy looked like declaring war; of waiting for a convoy to assemble in Liverpool and then sailing to Suez by the most roundabout route imaginable, by way of Freetown and Cape Town, Colombo and Bombay.

I was too young to realize that people are nearly always too busy to be much concerned about one's own affairs unless one is a positive nuisance to them or, more rarely, can be of some use. I need not have worried; a junior subaltern arriving in the middle of the night caused not a ripple. I was introduced to some officers sitting round a hurricane lamp in a large tent, given whisky and biscuits and despatched to my camp bed which somebody's kind batman had put up. In the morning I reported officially to the adjutant, Captain Noble, was told that I was to join C Company and was driven off in a 15 cwt. truck by Colin Kerr. Since the battalion was scattered over a wide area, that was the last I saw of headquarters for a long time.

It was a comfort to learn on the dusty, bumpy ride that Colin too was an E.C.O. or Emergency Commissioned Officer, a title whose various possible interpretations always tickled me, as had the fact that at Sandhurst in November 1939 we were the first batch of Cadets, hard on the heels of the last company of Gentlemen Cadets. Colin had worked for the Ottoman Bank in the Middle East before the war, and hence was ideally qualified both as mess treasurer and I.O. He tried to sort out my confusion of names and faces from the night before, and told me whom I would be meeting at C Company. He had, and has, a smile of great charm spreading widely across a smooth, unlined face and when he dropped me at the company, I knew there was at least someone I was going to like very much.

The track from battalion headquarters had wound up the Wadi el Naghamish, running inland towards a ridge whence presumably flowed the winter rains that had

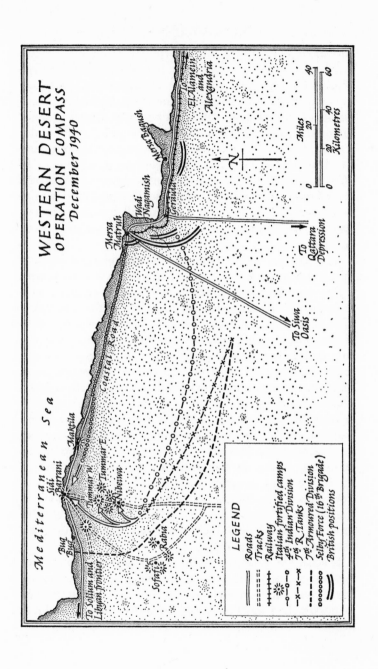

WESTERN DESERT
OPERATION COMPASS
December 1940

Mediterranean Sea

To Sollum and
Libyan Frontier

Bug
Bug
Sidi
Barrani
Maktila
Tummar W.
Tummar E.
Nibeiwa
Sofafi
Rabia
Coastal Road
Mersa
Matruh
Wadi
Nagamish
Mersa Bagush
Gerauili
El Alamein
and
Alexandria

To Siwa
Oasis

To
Qattara
Depression

N

Miles
0   20   40
Kilometres
0   20   40   60

LEGEND

Roads	
Tracks	
Railway	
Italian fortified camps	
4th Indian Division	
7th R. Tanks	
7th Armoured Division	
Selby Force (16th Brigade)	
British positions	

carved its bed. Along this escarpment stretched the forward companies, with C on the left. Well down the slope behind the crest was company headquarters, a sandbag hut that doubled as office and mess; the cookhouse, more sandbags but roofless, and what stores had been brought up to the forward positions. The company commander was Major Donald Bannerman, the second-in-command Lt. David Douglas, and that was our complement of officers. The Major, as I always called him even to myself since he seemed so unbelievably senior, told me I was to take over 15 Platoon, and my bed roll travelled the last few hundred yards of its 18,000-mile journey from Inverness.

The platoon and I took stock. Good manners hid any misgivings on their part, while I was too preoccupied with trying to learn their names to worry over making an instant fool of myself. The company commander and fellow officers do a fair amount in the instruction of a new subaltern, but the real educational drive comes from the company sergeant-major and the platoon sergeant; in our scattered layout it all depended on Sgt. Horbury of 15 Platoon. He was a little man, rather wizened after fifteen years' service, several broken teeth very apparent when he grinned, which was often, a skin turned dark yellow rather than brown by the sun. He looked as though he were recovering from jaundice, but never was there a less jaundiced nature. By tact, guile and suggestion he steered me in the right direction, headed me off when he could from idiocy (his thunderous silences were a textbook in themselves on How Not to Do It) and made me feel, very properly, that I was lucky to have come to the best platoon in the battalion.

It wasn't an enormous command—Sgt. Horbury; three section commanders, Corporals Norton, Edwards and MacLean; one lance-corporal, Hawley, and seventeen men. Attached was Pte. Morrison, a driver from the M.T. Section, with a small truck which carried picks and shovels and spare ammunition. The three sections each occupied a 'post', in fact a bare patch of ground about 150 yards apart, with platoon HQ behind them. Its presence was marked by the truck and four bed rolls; mine, Horbury's, Morrison's, and the platoon runner's who now doubled as my batman. In the circumstances, his duties in the latter role were nil.

It seemed a quiet and uneventful command, which was an agreeable change since my journey from Scotland to Egypt had been enlivened by the charge of a draft of sixty reservists of the Highland Light Infantry. They were hard cases, and everywhere I took my unruly flock, from Maryhill Barracks to France, from Cape Town to Bombay, there had been plenty to drink and plenty of trouble. Never have I known men who could get so puggled in a twinkling yet, somehow, still keep going. They were never 'ugly fou' ' and the trouble was of the conventional kind — 'see yon polisman, croon him', and another name would have to be struck from my nominal roll. It was a depleted draft that I handed over at Port Said to the 2nd H.L.I.

In contrast, the Camerons seemed a douce, well-behaved set of men with the added advantages of being, for the time being at least, in a stationary position and of being 'my lot' and not a temporary responsibility. True, there was no opportunity in our position to be anything but good; dissipation took the form of a very rare bottle of Egyptian beer with a strong flavour of onions.

I was told by the Major where we were and what we were doing. Italy had been in the war for several months, though the large Italian army concentrated on the Libyan frontier had not yet launched its expected invasion of Egypt. It was not until after the war that one learned the odds. Against the Italian army of some 160,000 men in Libya, Wavell had then about 36,000 troops in Egypt, British, New Zealand and Indian, soon to be joined by an Australian division. But even I could see at the time that the main task was the defence of Egypt and the Suez Canal, to safeguard the crucial supply of Middle Eastern oil and to keep open the short route to India and the Far East. Italy's airforce, her modern fleet and her massive army constituted, in the light of our then knowledge, a serious threat.

The British Western Desert Force under General O'Connor consisted of the 7th Armoured Division, patrolling the frontier, a garrison in Mersa Matruh and, along the Mediterranean coast, the 4th Indian Division, consisting at that time of only two brigades, 5th and 11th. In the Indian Army an infantry brigade comprised one British and two Indian battalions; and the 2nd Camerons with the 1st/6th Rajputana Rifles and the 4th/7th Rajput Regiment formed 11th Indian Infantry Brigade. Our role was to construct and then hold the Bagush 'Box', forcing an Italian invasion inland, away from the coastal road and railway line. Work on the Box—strongpoints linked by barbed wire and anti-tank wire—had been under way for about a month before I arrived.

There wasn't much to show for our efforts along the ridge. Under a thick layer of dusty earth was rock, and a huge effort with pick and shovel made very little dent in it. Section posts were therefore 'sangars', North-West Frontier style; banked-up rocks and earth formed a short, angled trench above ground level. We learned in later campaigns how effective they could be, but of course in the desert, except at blinding noon, they were all too visible, looking like the round barrows dotted over the Wessex downs. It was hard work putting them up, on a gallon and a half of water a day for all purposes—a princely ration, we realized later—and with no shade, but the sections kept at it cheerfully. The Jocks wore nothing much but identity discs, and a balmoral to keep the sun off; somewhere along the line topees or sun helmets had been slung away as lumber. I discarded mine as quickly and unobtrusively as possible, glad to be rid of the most awkward headgear ever devised by a military costumier. As children in the East, my sister and I were smacked if we ventured out without a topee, and it was heartening to find that the sun's lethal rays were a myth.

For any newcomer, routine once learned is a blessing, provided that there seems to be a purpose behind it; and here the routine was simple enough. The day started at 5 with stand-to at first light, however unlikely an Italian probe might be: some of the platoon's water was used for shaving: breakfast, like dinner and tea, was eaten centrally in shifts at the company cookhouse, where most o the water ration was kept. Back to sangar building, a stand-to at dusk and asleep by 8.30, with a round of the section posts some time in the middle of the night. The reason was to make sure that the sentry in each section was alert, and to let him know that he wasn't the only person on duty in the numbing silence of the desert night. There was no moon and an overcast sky my first few nights, and twice I got lost between the third section and platoon HQ; I hoped Horbury would ascribe my delayed return to painstaking zeal rather than incompetence.

We were allowed no lights at night, which cramped conviviality but produced some excellent conversation. Usually the sky was clear and it was enough entertainment to lie looking at the stars, with not even a glow at ground level to diminish the intensity of their light. It really was a 'spacious firmament on high'.

Soldiers have a genius for smoking unobtrusively; the fag would be lit, asphyxiatingly, under one's blanket, and then cupped between the hands. I once told the platoon, on parade, to put their hands out, palms up, and apart from those of the few non-smokers, every pair was clearly distinguished by a bright orange patch. But there was little of parades apart from the daily weapon inspection. In addition to rifle and bayonet, and my pistol, the platoon's armament consisted of three Bren guns, one in each section, a two-inch mortar and the anti-tank rifle. The Bren was an excellent weapon, capable of single-shot

7

or automatic fire, robust and trouble-free unlike the old Lewis gun it had replaced. The anti-tank rifle was a clumsy brute, very heavy, firing single rounds of what we hoped would prove armour-piercing ammunition. The gunner had to be a strong man to carry the thing, and it wasn't a popular job; Pte. Crowe had the muscle, and resignation if not enthusiasm.

Meals were an opportunity of getting to know the Major and David Douglas. Our food of course was whatever the company was eating. Bacon and fried bread was the invariable breakfast, while dinner and tea usually consisted of bully beef, sometimes deliquescent from the tin and sometimes cooked up with onions or potatoes, or else perfectly dreadful herrings in tomato sauce, a tepid, coagulated mass with no discernible connection with fish or vegetable. The occasional bone, we swore, was machine-made and inserted to give countenance to the label on the tin. And always, morning noon and night, delicious, sustaining, ever-refreshing army char.

At midday, the sweat pouring off us, char cooled us, while the same char stopped our teeth chattering at night; char kept the army going, through anything. Any quartermaster knew that whatever the circumstances he had to get the char ration—tea, sugar and condensed milk—and the ammunition up front; anything else could be sacrificed if the carrying party or the mules or the motor transport couldn't cope. With ammo and char, one was in business. The tea and the sugar arrived in the same sandbag, emptied into a dixie and boiled up together, and then in went the condensed milk. The brew, strong, sweet and scalding, was an elixir, no matter how one would dislike it now. Possibly some of its virtue lay in the faint flavour of sacking which lingered on one's palate.

The Company Office and mess consisted of a makeshift table and a box which contained the company whisky bottle, when we had one. Here we were waited on by the Major's batman, Lockie, who had been a Seaforth before transferring to the Camerons and was accordingly called by all the Jocks 'Caber Feidh', the Seaforth slogan. He was, I was told, a great shinty player, though the only athleticism he could display now was ducking in and out of the little sandbag hut. The Major reserved his few sallies of humour for Lockie, who gave as good as he got without ever stepping over the line; a Molière servant. Donald Bannerman was a very senior officer to be commanding a company. He had joined the regiment just at the end of the first war, and had the unusual distinction of being a fully qualified Russian interpreter. This stemmed from service in support of the White Russians, whence his story of visiting men's messes as Orderly Officer and asking the usual question, 'Any complaints?'

'Yes, sir,' said an incensed Jock with a dish of caviare, 'the jam tastes o' fush.'

He was never really well. We all suffered from desert sores, suppurating, boil-like excrescences on the arms and legs, as welcome as honey pots to the flies, but the Major was rotten with them and never stirred without an elegant flywhisk. He was very patient with me, but I learned more of my trade from David Douglas, the second-in-command.

It says a good deal about the 2nd Camerons, I realize when I look back, that it was a long time after I joined them that I learned, from him, that David had fairly recently been commissioned with two others in the battalion; he had been a CSM in another company. The fact was irrelevant to his fellow officers and to the warrant officers and NCOs he was now commanding; I can think of other regiments where this would not have been so. David's father had been in the regiment, and his brother was then in the 1st Battalion; he himself had joined as a boy-soldier and had served with the 2nd at home, in Palestine and in India. He was a professional soldier and a Cameron Highlander to his finger-tips, and worked hard to bring me up to something approaching the standard he thought necessary in second lieutenants. His method was

9

to instil the lesson, often with a ribald anecdote to adorn the tale; make sure you understood the reason for doing whatever it was; and then unmercifully tongue-lash you, in private, if you failed. It was highly effective, and turned him into a close friend for, so far, 37 years.

In many ways David epitomized the Camerons, although it was some time before I could begin to grasp the battalion as a corporate entity. Being scattered in company and even platoon detachments was a wonderful opportunity to get to know my own platoon and the rest of C Company; it would have taken ten times as long if we had been in barracks instead of living together in a small group. The disadvantage of course was that it took correspondingly longer to meet people in the other companies or in battalion HQ, with the exception of the Colonel, now back from leave and a regular inspector of his companies. Colin Cameron was a very alarming figure, particularly as I only saw him when I was in trouble.

Fired by Donald Bannerman's vivid description of C Company's position being, almost, in the front line, and most certainly being so when the expected enemy advance took place, I had pushed ahead as fast as possible with the building of my three little sangars, which generated a very competitive spirit in the sections. Unfortunately the C.O. was giving no prizes for speed. Neatness was all, and here 15 Platoon fell down lamentably. Our stones were piled up higgledy-piggledy, the rubble of the infilling was tight-packed but untidy, and the earth banked up as a facing was asymmetrical.

'What is this supposed to be?'

'A sangar, sir.'

'You must be *mad*, Cochrane. It is a mess. Take it down and rebuild it properly.'

Three days later Brigadier Savory came round: 'Must get these positions finished, run up the sangar as fast as you can.' But the brigadier was a distant Jove, his blessings or thunderbolts too remote to affect a platoon commander, while the C.O. was an immediate terror, like a leaking gas main in the kitchen.

He was a taciturn man. One day he drove up the slope in his car to the platoon area, so I doubled over to see what had gone wrong this time.

'Get in', and he told his driver to go through the wire, in which there were gaps but, in those primitive days, no mines. We wheeled right, along the ridge towards our neighbours, the Rajputana Rifles, bumping along and creating a delicious breeze inside the car and a huge cloud of dust behind.

'Get out'; and we looked at the Raj Rif busy building their sangars in a position similar to our own; unlike the Jocks, the sepoys were very properly dressed in their pale blue, rather thick shirts and khaki shorts, topped by the neat Rajput turban.

'Get in', and back we went to our own lines.

I learned more about the ground in front of our position by patrolling. This entailed taking a corporal and two or three men through the wire and south for some miles, swinging west and coming back through Don or D Company's wire. (In signalese, the rifle companies were Ack, Beer, Charlie and Don. Later in the war the first four letters of the alphabet became Able, Baker, Charlie, Dog.) One had to be careful over compass bearings and in the judgement of distance which was often a tedious business of counting paces. We seldom found anything, certainly no enemy; once or twice we bumped into an encampment of Senussi bedouin, driven out of their territory on the Libyan frontier by the advancing Italians, and drifting quietly eastward with their camels and goats. Once however we saw an orange-red glow on the horizon; an enemy armoured car or truck on fire? I set off briskly towards it, and was gratified to see it steadily growing and brightening as we marched on. Finally Corporal MacLean broke silence with a polite cough.

'D'ye see yon, sir?'

'Well, of course, we're heading for it.'

'Well, I'm thinking it's no' anything on fire, sir, I'm thinking it's the moon.' And so it was, which led to some salty jokes in the company next day.

It felt, paradoxically, a very lonely life sometimes, despite the fact that I was never away from the platoon except for the half-hour meal in the company mess, and I often longed for someone to whom I could blow off steam when I felt depressed, especially after a rasping from the C.O. On the other hand, I could console myself with the thought that, for better or worse, 15 Platoon and I were getting to know one another pretty well.

The desert was full of surprises. To start with, I enjoyed the fact that it was the Western Desert—at that time, this correct topographical term was confined to the army, and hadn't reached the newspapers. West has always been a conjurative word, from the Western Isles to 'Westren wind, when wilt thou blow?'; I should have disliked being in an Eastern Desert. Then, it wasn't sandy, and it wasn't flat, and had clearly once been inhabited and cultivated, indeed was still cultivable; one night we found a shallow wadi with a few gourds still growing, the remains of someone's planting after the previous winter's rains. Here and there we came across underground cisterns, like stone-lined ship's decanters; who built them, and how did the rain fill them up through the narrow neck?

There was little wild life; birds like swifts, plenty of small scorpions and a few snakes, and one or two chameleons. 9 Section captured a very large one which changed colour satisfyingly, although the Cameron tartan defeated it. It eventually settled on a muddy brown and sulked, its throat pulsing indignantly, until it was given a taste of bully beef and its freedom. The desert was full of colour, at least early in the morning and at dusk, with pink and orange tints shading into violet and deepest indigo. Only at white-glaring noon, and when vehicles cut up the crust into dense, clinging yellow clouds of dust did it really merit the famous Australian description of 'miles and miles of shit-coloured f—— all'.

I had any amount of advice when I enlisted, but the only sensible counsel came from Maurice Bowra, when I said goodbye after clearing out my rooms at Wadham: 'I know you won't shirk danger, dear boy, but do, I implore you, avoid discomfort like the plague.' However excellent, it was not easy advice to follow, for one couldn't wash the dust off. Larded with sweat, it formed an adhesive paste which in time dried and crumbled, ready for the next layer; the sort of mudpack, one supposed, which in different surroundings cost a great deal of money.

Relief came only when we were taken down in detachments to the sea. Never mind that the return journey by truck left one just as dirty as before, the half-hour of splashing and swimming was glorious. We thought ourselves in clover when the Indian sappers actually brought the sea water to us; they came to build a pillbox to supplement the sangars, with a tank of water to mix the concrete. The platoon had a daily dip until the water turned too muddy. The water ration was soon cut to half a gallon, so we grew steadily filthier.

The company position was now ready, although I am glad it was never put to the test. 15 Platoon was accordingly sent one day to complete some half-finished sangars near the shore for the Central India Horse, the divisional recce battalion, and we had a splendid day out. Rather than an imposition, the dreary chore of working for another unit was a lark, since John Connell, the company quartermaster sergeant, had been liberal with the rations. The Jocks dug like fury and then we had a stormy bathe while the dixie brewed up; tinned salmon, with bread and jam, was a Lucullan meal because it was a picnic. On the way back we found an abandoned field of pumpkins and crammed twenty-eight into the truck to give the company a fresh vegetable. If pumpkins had been issued in the ration, there would have been a near-mutiny, but to have

13

them as finder's keeper's was another lark, and so everyone ate the repellent thing. This Boys' Brigade outing was my first taste of the delights of independent command; major-general and corporal alike feel a heady exhilaration in being ordered to do something away from the immediate control of a superior.

All this seemed very far from the war. Mail took a long time to arrive from home, but we knew of the pulverizing night raids on London and the great cities of Britain. A cable from my parents to say all was well left one thinking 'So far, yes: but how long can they stand this?' All we saw of action were some heavy bombing attacks on Mersa Matruh, and dog fights in which the R.A.F. in Gladiator biplanes shot down four Italian fighters. This activity was to cover a major enemy advance to the fishing village of Sidi Barrani. The Italian claim that after conquering it they had got its tramcars running again gave much pleasure. It began to look as though the war might be hotting up in Egypt. Fighting patrols and listening patrols were out every night, which was hard work since David had been sent off to a field engineering course and I found myself second-in-command as well as 15 Platoon commander. There was a perk in the shape of a tent at company HQ, though it was a conceptual luxury rather than an actual one since alternate nights were spent as duty officer by the telephone or on patrol.

The sangars were finished, and the Box defensible, we hoped, so the C.O. decided it was time for some battalion training after our couple of months' digging and building. We advanced and retired, wheeled and countermarched in desert formation, the companies spread out in a vast diamond marked by a pillar of cloud kicked up by the carrier platoon and the trucks. We did communications exercises, both wireless and visual. The latter meant not only lamp and helio but large blue and red flags waved from the C.O.'s car, indicating I forget what. Wireless in those days consisted of a heavy, clumsy contraption carried by the company signaller, in contact with battalion HQ; platoon to company communications were by runner. We moved in daylight by sun compass, something like a sundial fixed to the wing of a truck, and by night on compass bearings; we moved in transport and, very good for our legs, we marched and marched and marched. I was modestly proud of my ability to cover the ground, and felt the more ashamed at a prolonged attack of gippy tummy which compelled me to fall out frequently; no kindly hedges, but I felt so weak and ill that the absurdity of squatting beside the line of march in the sole cover of my own shadow never entered my head.

The training exercises gave me an opportunity to see something of the other companies. At that time a battalion's official establishment was twenty-two officers and 646 other ranks. Headquarter Company included the signals platoon; the anti-aircraft platoon whose A.A.-mounted bren guns were supposed to drive off dive bombers; the three-inch mortar platoon which was our own private artillery; the carrier platoon, with ten lightly armoured tracked carriers, each carrying a bren gun; the pioneer platoon, whose worst job was always that of clearing mines; and the admin platoon, ruled over by the Quartermaster, and the Transport Officer with his fifty or so drivers.

There were four rifle companies, supposed to have three officers each, one of whom was a platoon commander. The other two platoons in each company were commanded by platoon-sergeant-majors, in the case of C Company by PSMs Bain and Galloway. 'Chucky' Bain was a neat, precise, irascible-looking man, distinguished by the ribbon of the Military Medal which he had been awarded in Palestine, and soon to be commissioned. Galloway was heavily built, with an easy-going air; he had been a gardener at Loretto before enlisting, though ahead of my time there. In fact, their looks belied them, the one being even-tempered, the other a good disciplinarian, so far as I could tell from 15 Platoon. The army must have decided that PSMs were not a good idea, for eventually all platoons were commanded by officers when they were available.

At the apex of the pyramid was Battalion HQ which consisted of the Commanding Officer and Second-in-Command; the Adjutant, who is the C.O.'s staff officer, with his Orderly Room clerks; the Intelligence Officer with half a dozen men; and of course the awe-inspiring figure of the Regimental Sergeant Major. Finally, attached to headquarters was the Medical Section of twenty stretcher bearers, who in fact were converted bandsmen. Brass instruments are all very well for stirring the martial emotions in peacetime, but are out of place on active service, whereas the pipes were never left behind. Each company had its piper, and with luck more than one.

Whether or not it is the case in other countries, it is a fact that the British do not like being part of a mass. We seem unable to attach ourselves to or find an identity in a group larger than, say, eight hundred or so. This is as true of schools or factories as it is in the services. The size of a battalion is no accident, for it is planned to produce that feeling of 'belonging' without which no organization can prosper.

I learned during these exercises that when the C.O. was displeased, which was often since he was a stickler for correctness, he would address his company commanders as briskly as me, and I felt less keenly the imperfections of 15 Platoon's sangars. I also began to learn what a really good regular unit could do with a minimum of fuss and bawling. As a schoolboy in the thirties I had absorbed the conventional wisdom that the regular army was officered by a coterie of elderly Blimps with a leaven of frivolous young men whose only occupations were riding or shooting. A weekly parade in the school O.T.C. and a week's camp every year didn't do anything to change the imagined picture; in any case we had all read Graves and Sassoon, Remarque and Brooke and Blunden, though I doubt if anyone at Loretto was reading Owen at that time. Oxford in 1938–39, with Munich and the debate on conscription, made one start thinking a little about the stereotype, since war was clearly on the way.

Mine was not a militaristic family—my father never spoke of his experiences in France between 1915 and 1918 —but Hitler was looked on as unrelievedly evil by my parents. I suppose I had decided at Oxford, without consciously thinking of it, that when the inevitable happened I would enlist without waiting to be called up, and in the army because I didn't like machinery. When war did break out, to join up and try to get into the Cameron Highlanders, my father's regiment in the first War, took no thought, but I still had a very cloudy notion of the army I was joining, beyond the fact that it was probably crass and bumbling.

Newspapers and television are blamed, usually rightly, for purveying the easily accepted view, of passing on and helping to create the current cant, in Johnson's sense of the word. This is nothing new, and in the thirties the cant about the army was on a level with the cant about the empire, both sitting targets for the easy witticism. How smart one was to laugh at institutions so inherently ludicrous!

But in the summer of 1940 the army consisted for me of C Company in very sharp focus, with the battalion in rather smudgier outline beyond. It consisted of men who had been soldiers for years, tough, good at their job, professionals through and through. They were in the main agreeable as individuals but formidable en bloc; assuredly they weren't ludicrous. And the desert was on altogether too large a scale for clever mockery; scope for passions in the grand manner, no doubt, scope too for laughter, but not for the smart snigger at unapprehended values.

Before recent amalgamations changed the pattern, an infantry regiment consisted of two battalions, one usually overseas and the other at home, each fed with recruits from the regimental depot. Cardwell, Secretary for War in 1868–74, had created this system by linking two of the old regiments of foot, which retained their original numbers, and by building a depot for the resulting new regiment, which accounts for the wondrously variegated range of late Victorian military architecture to be found in so many county towns. Thus when a Sandhurst friend, Dickie La Croze, who was French and determined to wear tartan, was commissioned in the H.L.I., he went to see his peacetime employers in the City. Seeing his brand new uniform, a commissionaire darted out of a doorway asking, '71st or 74th, sir?'—the original numbers of the 1st and 2nd Battalions. Dickie had barely started to read up his regimental history, and could only reply, helpfully, 'I don't think either of those buses comes along here.'

The Queen's Own Cameron Highlanders, the 79th Foot, was unique in that a second battalion was raised from scratch to form the link, and it too was numbered the 79th. In recent years the 2nd Battalion had served in Egypt and Palestine, then in India before returning to Egypt in 1939, while the 1st Battalion had gone to France with the British Expeditionary Force, had come out through Dunkirk and was later to distinguish itself in Burma.

I suppose there were few in C Company with as long service as the Major, though Wattie Reid, the CSM, and John Connell, the CQMS, must have run him close; but five, seven and ten years' service was commonplace. In a well-led unit, a man can hardly help becoming a good soldier with that much experience behind him. Officers and men knew each other through and through, weaknesses as well as strengths, which could have made a newcomer's arrival as frosty as gatecrashing a successful party. It didn't, largely because of the company's determination to turn a chance subaltern into a 2nd Battalion man. Regimental feeling was strong, though never overtly expressed except in connection with football or tug o' war competitions; it emerged from the many yarns, told as we sat in the dark, about men and happenings, sometimes serious and sometimes funny. The stories were by no means all to the glory of the regiment, but the assumption was very clear that so-and-so had behaved well (often, in the funny stories, in highly unmilitary circumstances) because he was a Cameron, while somebody else earned the damning epithet of being a bad soldier because he wasn't worth his place in the regiment.

There was frequently a family link. Toby Irvine, the Transport Officer, had to find a new driver for the C.O., not the easiest vacancy to fill, and promoted Pte. MacGuire to lance corporal, with the job. MacGuire's comment was that 'my grandfather was a private in the Camerons, and my father was a private in the Camerons —it takes three generations of MacGuires to get to be a lance corporal'. But there was no need to be a Highlander or even a Scot to become imbued with the regimental feeling; Sgt. Horbury had abandoned barrow-pushing in Stepney fifteen years earlier to enlist and had fetched up more or less by chance in the Camerons, but I learned almost more from him about what made the regiment function than anybody. Alas, I couldn't learn the precision and sure-footed neatness that had made him a champion highland dancer in the regiment and in the Highland Brigade.

It would have been interesting to know men's reasons for enlisting when there appeared to be no family tradition to bring them into the regiment, but it would have been a most impertinent question. Pte. Morrison, the platoon driver, did once tell me his reason, succinctly: 'I was awfu' hungry.'

Service in India had left its mark, from luxuriant tattooing and a patois studded with Urdu words to the fact that we still had two Indian cooks in the company. They suffered more than we did as the winter cold set in, and I am sure they had not bargained on being involved in actual warfare, but they cooked away cheerfully in all conditions. All the Jocks used a sprinkling of Arabic and Indian words, and it was a lingo one had to master to understand half of what was being said. 'Jildhi now wi' your piallas, conner's up', meant doubling with enamel mugs because food was ready; water was always *pani*, a hurricane lamp was a *buttee*—the list was a long one. After *wadi*, the commonest Arabic words were *malesh*—it doesn't matter—and, in reminiscence or anticipation, *bint* meaning a girl.

For leave had re-started, with three or four men sent away at a time to leave camps at Alex or Cairo. Great was my jubilation at being sent off for six days, which meant four whole days at the Continental Hotel in Cairo. There was no other officer from the battalion on leave then, but I bumped into friends from other regiments, in particular Michael Cooper-Clarke of the 11th Hussars, and so didn't lack for company. The principal attraction of Cairo, of course, was the feeling of being clean once more; one couldn't have enough water, in the shape of baths at the hotel or swimming at the Gezira Club. Next came the pleasures of the table; a good dinner made one realize how boring was a steady diet of bully beef. Third, I think, was walking about amongst the people of the city, all busy on their own affairs and not concerned in soldiering, which was good for one's sense of proportion.

Michael and I paid the obligatory visit to the Pyramids. In the city itself bookshops were the magnet; the worst deprivation in the desert was reading matter, and I was starving for print. I found very little because pre-war stocks had nearly all been sold, but I got a Penguin *Antigua Penny Puce* and a *Discours sur la Méthode* (Descartes in French in the desert was to prove a slow read) and a World's Classic called, I think, *The Lonely Plough*. Just because this *was* a book, I came to think it a good book and sang its praises in letters home. Years later I learned that my parents had in consequence read it and each concluded privately that dysentery or heat had addled my brain.

A bunch of us spent our evenings in cinemas or a night club, open-eyed at the contortions of the resident belly dancer; I could easily take on trust the legend that her muscles and her agility enabled her to crack a walnut in her navel. My diary ruefully notes that I spent no less than £20 in four days, a fortune for a second lieutenant in 1940. After buying a huge basket of fruit to take back to the company and paying my hotel bill, I found I could either dine or drink while waiting for the train. Cairo bars were generous in the small eats they provided, so I opted for drinking, though I was pretty hungry by the time I got back to the cookhouse. After only two and a half months with C Company, it felt like coming home.

2

DESERT ACTION

IT was in October that we had what the books call our
first brush with the enemy. As a military operation it
was a fiasco, but it was invaluable for us all to learn at
little risk that mere noise isn't lethal; and to the tyro, it is
the noise of the battlefield that is disconcerting, and hence
frightening. The battalion was to make a raid on an
enemy position near Sidi Barrani, presumably to demonstrate to the Italians that our defence of Egypt wasn't
merely passive. David Douglas was still away on his
course, but Alan Cameron joined C Company in his
place, returning to the battalion from a job at divisional
HQ. We set off in lorries on the 21st, driving for eight
hours and bivouacing for the night; next day we had our
orders—a two-company attack, C and D left and right,
on what was supposed to be a motorized Libyan battalion
entrenched in the Wadi el Maktila, with the sea to the
north and the Sidi Barrani–Mersa Matruh road to the
south. We were to inflict what damage we could to
vehicles, take prisoners and then get out. The road was
our start line, held for us for the evening by the Rifle
Brigade; and just before midnight we crossed it.

Our arrival was scarcely a surprise, since the gunners
had shelled the camp for three hours, and D Company
bumped a post almost at once, going in with the bayonet.
The shouting and firing led the Major to swing us round
to support them; it died down and we got back on our
original line, with the object of breaking into the camp
near the sea, taking some prisoners and smashing up
vehicles. Changing direction in the dark, when ground
hasn't been reconnoitred in daylight, is a muddling affair,

and we were just getting sorted out when we were seen, or heard, and everything opened up. We dived on our bellies, and lay watching an aurora borealis of tracer whistling over us—red, white and blue. It was unnerving until we realized that nobody was being hit, but I think we were all frightened at first by the din which sounded highly dangerous. The officer always has the best of it on these occasions because he has the most to do and least leisure to think awkward thoughts; getting the platoon together and on down the wadi kept me busy enough.

It is remarkable how much ammunition can be wasted at night; the Germans in Italy used to shoot off almost as much as did the Italians in Egypt and in East Africa. The British were either better disciplined or less plentifully supplied.

We were held up again by a machine gun firing on a fixed and well chosen line. The Major told me to take a patrol down the wadi to see what was what; I called for three volunteers, and for the first time felt the enormous satisfaction of having the whole of 15 Platoon come forward. We found nothing, as I reported: and the Major issued fresh orders to Alan Cameron and me, as the three of us lay with our heads together under the canopy of tracer. It wasn't only our heads—Alan and I had our revolvers in our hands, and the Major suddenly realized that both weapons were pointing in his face, inches away. It was one of the few occasions I saw Donald Bannerman really angry.

'Put those damned things away, they're dangerous.' He decided, wisely, to get into the camp from our present position rather than nearer the sea, so off we went toward the source of all the shooting, which had now largely died away.

On the skyline we could see some dark blobs which we took to be enemy positions: the Major sent 14 and 15 Platoons in. I felt more and more blue as I plodded on, the platoon, with fixed bayonets, spread behind and alongside me, moving by sections, the Italians still holding their fire. It seemed the moment to close the gap quickly, so self-consciously I shouted 'Charge!' and we broke into a double. But distance at night is deceptive, and after running for what felt like ten minutes with the dark blobs getting larger and larger, I was winded; so the two platoons eventually arrived at a slow lope. Our objective turned out to be a neatly parked row of eight big lorries.

We had some picks and a sledge-hammer, and molotov cocktails, and set about the lorries, making a row like a mad blacksmith's forge; one was a big water tanker, all the taps of which we turned on. No enemy fire, indeed no enemy apart from two Libyans hiding under a lorry: but I knew this was too good to last, and that we were a vulnerable crowd. To his fury, I sent Horbury back to the company with most of the two platoons, keeping PSM Bain and half a dozen men. I got one of our prisoners (we lost the other in the confusion) into the cab of the only undamaged vehicle while Chucky set fire to the water lorry and two others loaded with petrol and ammunition. The moment the Libyan started up the engine, a very noisy diesel, the firing started in earnest. We found we were in a crescent of enemy posts, and were a very good target in the moonlight even after we had drawn away from the burning lorries.

We didn't draw away very fast, since our prisoner, it turned out, wasn't a real driver, and could find no gear higher than bottom, so Chucky and the Jocks had to walk rather slowly alongside to keep pace. I was kneeling on the passenger seat with my pistol against the poor prisoner's head, in an over-dramatic way; at one point he stopped completely, to beg for mercy, I suppose; to my shame, I belted him in the face, to urge him to proceed, while Pte. Smith on the running-board belted him too, just for luck. We rumbled on, the enemy fire much too accurate to be comfortable. They were now shooting tracer anti-tank shells at us; two whistled through the canvas hood and one skipped over the bonnet just in front of the windscreen.

I reckoned we would never manage to ride back, and would have to walk it, so we abandoned our lorry after wrecking it and putting a match to it. We set off with our Libyan and some papers and maps, no doubt merely mechanic's instructions and tourist maps of Egypt, and a water bottle filled with Chianti. We discovered that this was so after offering it to our prisoner, who took a swig and spat it out in disgust, muttering 'Islam'. We marched by the compass and finally hit the main road where we bumped into Colin Kerr, who took me to the C.O.; I reported, and we marched back to our transport along the white tape which had guided us to the start line hours earlier. I found I was soaking in sweat and very tired.

The result was pretty meagre— eight lorries destroyed and one prisoner taken, with two enemy killed, for four killed on our side; and I doubt whether the prisoner imparted any useful information. Our casualties were all in D Company, apart from one man missing from 14 Platoon. However, it was an exceptionally good field exercise for us; fortunate is the unit whose first blooding is exciting and relatively painless, and which can learn the correct lessons, particularly in a night operation. But it took a long time for Sgt. Horbury to forgive me.

The only disagreeable consequence was being ordered to talk to a war correspondent, and to read subsequently his inflation of the affair into a brilliantly conceived and executed operation. A Highland regiment always seems to have an unfortunate effect on journalists, and presumably in 1940 almost anything had to be dressed up as a success; but this twaddle was enough to make us the laughing stock of the division, who knew what had really happened. I was in a state of embarrassed misery about it, but fortunately no one seemed to believe that I had told the man what he had written.

Back at the Bagush Box we carried on with training and

night exercises, in which we now saw a good deal more point, but life was fairly easy since we had finished work on the posts, and the dawn and dusk stand-to's were dropped. Wattie Reid, as befitted a CSM of his service and standing, exacted a high standard from his NCOs and hence from C Company, with a nice discrimination between what was sensible and what would have been absurd in our situation. One evening he explained to me that spit and polish, as a mindless aim, could be counter-productive.

'In Hawick, where I come frae, I kent a man wi' a truly fearsome wife who kept the hoose beezed up past a' enduring, he couldna' even step in the back door wi' his boots on, an' she was aye at him for messing up the hoose by living in it. Weel, the front room was her joy, naebody could get intae it unless the meenister called for tea, an' her pride in the front room was the fireplace, a' black-leaded an' shining. Poor man, it was nae life, but a' week he'd put up wi' it, till Saturday. Then he'd get fou, every Saturday he'd get fou, and every Saturday night he'd come home an' march intae the front room an' he'd feel a real man, an' he'd oot and he'd piss all over that fireplace. So you see, Mr. Cochrane, it doesna' do to have too much of a good thing in the wrong place, even beezing up.'

David returned to the company and I found myself no longer the junior officer of the battalion when 2nd. Lt. Robertson arrived to take command of 14 Platoon. We contrived to amuse ourselves with company sing-songs sitting around under the stars, the repertoire ranging from the sentimental to *The Ball of Kirriemuir*. And I was introduced to the complications of euchre, played by the light of a hurricane lamp in the mess after supper. We said goodbye to the Major who left the battalion on posting to a staff job, and then to Alan Cameron who returned to divisional HQ. David took over C Company, and a wonderful commander he proved, tough as old boots on parade or in action, a very good friend when we were off duty.

At a higher level, Colonel Cameron left us in November after a tremendous week of non-stop exercises; it was thanks to him that the 2nd Camerons was so highly trained a unit. His successor, Lt. Col. Anderson, had been the second-in-command. Andy was a great man and a very fine soldier, both in command of the battalion and later the brigade. A regular Cameron Highlander, he was commissioned in the field and decorated in World War I, so he was no longer a young man. But he was as hardy as any of us, and overflowing with a cheerful zest and energy that ran through the entire unit. Of middle height, crinkled greyish hair, a rubicund face and a merry eye, he had a rapid speech, as though he was thinking faster than he could utter. He was the best of all disciplinarians, absolutely fair and absolutely strict, and all ranks thought the world of him. We knew we had a colonel like nobody else's.

To descend again to my level, I was very happy with 15 Platoon. The three corporals had all been sensible at Maktila, and had kept control of their sections during the messing about in the dark, and several of the men had showed initiative, in particular Patterson, Matthews and 37 Smith. The first was a big fellow, and big men are usually good leaders or sheepish followers, with no intermediate grade; Matthews was a scruffy-looking Jock with no obvious qualities until he was under pressure, while Smith was one of the company hard cases, and a very likeable one.

We had several of them, and—in peacetime stations —drink had always been the trouble. A soldier had two essential documents, his pay book which listed, as well as his pay, the basic information the army required of all its members, which may be summarized as name, rank, number, religion and size of boots. The other was his conduct sheet, endorsed with the results of any conflict with military authority, and in red ink for serious offences. Corporal MacKintosh in 14 Platoon, for instance, had leaf after leaf of conduct sheet recording promotions, convictions, reductions to the ranks, and subsequent promotions; and 37 Smith's sheets too were a river of red ink, though they didn't record any promotions. (A soldier with a common name always had the last two digits of his regimental number prefixed to it. As well as Smiths, we had of course a multitude of Camerons, Macdonalds and MacKenzies; there was an unfortunate signaller attached to D Company whose number ended 0000 and who was universally and even semi-officially known as F——all MacKenzie.) For someone like Smith, active service far from a wet canteen or the delights of 'gaein' doon the toon' was a chance to show what a good soldier he could be.

Another embarrassing reflection of the Maktila raid was the news that I had been awarded the M.C. as a consequence — embarrassing because it had been such a flop, and because I had done no more than PSM Bain; though also, but inwardly, very pleasing as the battalion's first medal in this war.

It was clear that we wouldn't go on sitting quietly in our position; the enemy had to come at us, or we had to go at him. More aerial activity seemed to indicate the former —a few bombs were dropped near us, and we watched a series of dog-fights in which the old Gladiators did well, shooting down nine Italian planes for the loss of four. But there was no sign of a forward move by Graziani's land forces, and our armoured cars and the Rifle Brigade were increasingly audacious in their aggressive patrolling around and between the big lagers or camps where the Italians were holed up. Although we did not know it, Wavell was ready to take the initiative.

When a commander pulls off a big double, one leg an apparent walkover, he is seldom given credit for the audacity of the coup; yet Wavell's plan was singularly bold. He was already committed to sending a British force to Greece, but in November 1940 he decided to take the offensive in the desert, employing the depleted 7th

Armoured Division and its Support Group, the 4th Indian with its two brigades, and 16th Infantry Brigade, a British formation. I don't suppose even he foresaw how successful this attack would prove, but at the beginning of December, before he even launched it, he had already planned to switch the 4th Indian, after the initial assault, to the Sudan and replace it with the 6th Australian to carry on the good work in the desert while he opened a new campaign in Eritrea and Ethiopia. The Italian armies were to be smashed in north and east Africa before he had to deal with the Germans.

* * *

On December 5th we were warned that we were moving, lock stock and barrel, on a two-day corps exercise, and duly lumbered along all day on the 6th in three-ton lorries from the Royal Indian Army Service Corps, bivouacing and brewing-up just before dusk. Next day we had our true orders, which had been kept a total secret, even in Cairo, that hotbed of gossip. David came back with the C.O.'s orders and called in his platoon commanders, with Wattie Reid and John Connell. He told us that the army was going over to the attack, that 4th Indian was to wipe out the big Italian camps at Nibeiwa and Tummar and that the Camerons and Rajputana Rifles of 11th Brigade were to kick off by capturing Nibeiwa. He then gave us his detailed orders for the operation. Because C Company was to be the leading assault company, we really felt in 15 Platoon that we were the spearhead of Britain's first land offensive.

Unlike Maktila, there was to be no softening-up of the defences in advance of the infantry assault. The artillery would only shoot-up the camp in the few minutes at first light when the tanks were advancing, which demanded instant accuracy from the gunners, while C Company had to be in among the enemy within five minutes at most of the leading tank. I did not realize until much later that this plan, devised by General O'Connor who commanded the whole desert operation, stood conventional military wisdom on its head. It worked like a charm.

We made a minor move in daylight on Sunday the 8th and set off in earnest in the early evening, the noses of the big three-tonners rising and dipping in the sea of dust like a school of porpoises. The Indian drivers were excellent, particularly when the dusk had faded into night and only sidelights relieved the total darkness. My perk as platoon commander was to sit in the cab, and I found the little red tail light of the lorry in front hypnotic; it seemed to dim and brighten until, if I had been driving, I should have smashed into it. At dawn we found ourselves at precisely the right spot, with 30 'Infantry' tanks in front of us and the enemy camp ahead. We followed the tanks some way, the only occasion we got a lift right up to the battle, before we jumped out of the lorries, and legged it. It was also the only battle in which our company piper piped us into action, because it was the only one on flat enough ground to leave a piper sufficient breath to fill his bag.

In fact it was no battle for 15 Platoon, whose orders were to breach the perimeter, which consisted of ineffective wire and a ring of gun emplacements and infantry posts, and work up some 400 yards to the right while 14 Platoon did likewise to the left. I had two sections abreast, either side of me, with Horbury and the third section following, and can remember shouting like a madman to encourage myself as we jumped and scrambled over the wire. There was some shooting as we rushed three or four posts, Patterson bayoneting a machine-gunner. Another machine gun opened up rather too close to be pleasant, but one of the carriers dashed up and fixed it; we had only one casualty in the platoon, Pte. Francis, with a bullet in his shoulder. So we sat in our position, an Italian A.A. battery, and watched the rest of the battalion and the

Raj Rifs move through the gap and fan out into the camp. The combination of the tanks—antediluvian by later standards but bigger than anything the Italians had — and complete surprise meant that there was no serious resistance. The commander, Maletti, had been killed by a tank shell; we noticed later that the Italians were often very well led, but couldn't hold together if their commander were killed. Some 3,000 prisoners were taken.

I had sent a runner back to David after our assault, and he soon had the company organized and consolidated. It was then we heard that 14 Platoon had been less fortunate; Robbie, in command, and Corporal MacKintosh had been killed, and Sgt. Cairns wounded. This was bad news, for I had come to like Robbie very much, while Tosh was one of the company's real characters. It was only later that one absorbed news like this; at the moment there was worry about the next step, and an ebbing excitement, and a threatened counter-attack from the next camp, Tummar. But 5th Brigade of the division dealt with it as we had Nibeiwa, so we sat about in our A.A. battery eating Italian tinned fruit and envying whoever would have the pickings of the camp, which was crammed with material of every description. I had to be sharp over the wine and brandy, lying about in abundance.

It had been cold all day, and at night it was bitterly so. Shorts and shirt and a jersey are not the kit for winter in the desert. Our greatcoats were with our kilts and heavy baggage in Cairo, presumed unnecessary by the powers-that-be who should have known more about the climate, though this was the only lapse in the meticulous staff work of the campaign. It was bad enough for us, but must have been agony for the Indian sepoys.

Next day the prisoners were marched off in a long column and we were set to the nauseous task of burying the enemy dead. These were the first bodies that I, at least, had to handle; I don't believe we ever became so inured to corpses that we could treat those stuffed-doll

31

figures as mere lumber of the battlefield. A dead man in war seems so finally dead that it required an effort of the mind to realize that a few minutes earlier he too had been alive, and frightened, and hoping that his number wasn't on a bullet. I was never to get used to the terrible lack of dignity in nearly all the bodies; it seemed in a muddled way that if one had to be killed, one had the right to die decently and not be left lying about in a posture that too often could only be described as ludicrous. The pathetic was easier to bear— the young man, for instance, doubled back over a gun barrel, letters and snapshots of his girl spilling from an unbuttoned pocket. Ludicrous or pathetic, hideously mutilated or clean killed, they were our fellows though in an unfamiliar uniform, and they had to be buried. But I drew the line at extracting the charred remains of men from burnt-out tanks. That was a sight which led to nightmares.

Aircraft raided the camp, but left us alone in favour of bombing and machine-gunning our B Echelon—the battalion transport and non-fighting men like the cooks, always left a little behind the action. In the midst of this we were urgently ordered to load up in the lorries, and drove off to the western side of Sidi Barrani.

It had been attacked that morning by 16th Brigade, which had been attached to the division, at that time consisting only of two Indian brigades. The attack had been a partial success, and 11th Brigade had been switched at very short notice to complete the job. Our orders in the late afternoon were sudden and brief: all that Andy could tell David was that 'the Camerons will take Sidi Barrani, the tanks may be on our left and the Queen's on our right; the Argylls got heavy casualties this morning attacking it and the Leicesters were badly cut up. A Company leads, C follows.' So in we went with the bayonet after A, hoping to find an objective. We got as far as the village itself, which had been shelled to fragments, and then came under heavy machine-gun and artillery fire from our left. Where there's fire there's enemy, so we swung left, A with a flank on the shore, C up what appeared to be the middle of the camp. It was a very large area, and the companies and platoons were soon scattered as the advance surged on. 15 Platoon rushed three little hillocks from which fire was coming, and then stumbled into a maze of dugouts or camouflaged emplacements. I fell through the roof of one as far as my armpits just as Horbury pitched a grenade into its entrance. It is amazing how athletic acute fear can make one; I came out of that roof like a champagne cork, and just in time.

I had been using my revolver rather freely though quite ineffectively. My batman must have been counting the shots, for as the hammer clicked on an empty chamber he said, 'Run out, sir? Try this,' and like a loader at a big shoot handed me an Italian automatic.

Crowe, the anti-tank rifleman, was killed by a bullet in the head but otherwise we were undamaged despite all the shooting. As we took prisoners we sent them back, though where they went I've no idea; however, we now bumped into a colossal column of prisoners—2,800 we found later—escorted by Wattie Reid and half a dozen men. It was dusk; in all the hullaballoo I had lost touch with A Company and the rest of C, and there seemed to be no more enemy around, so I took the whole party south, towards the main road. We reached it just as the moon rose, floodlighting a deep anti-tank ditch which made a good pen for the prisoners. We sat them down in it, while Wattie and the men patrolled up an down the road; and I set off with a Jock to find someone to take the Italians over.

I made for Barrani village, thinking battalion HQ might be there, in which I was right, but found no officers. I commandeered a truck, and went back to find the prisoners, but they had gone. I was a very unhappy and freezing cold subaltern—I had lost my platoon and my company, in fact I had lost myself. I did find the Argylls, whose C.O. gave me a dram to stop my teeth rattling and whose medical officer was still working by hurricane lamps to save some of the casualties they had incurred in the morning.

I gave up after this, went back to the village, where HQ was by now functioning, and reported. Tony Noble, the adjutant, passed orders through me to the company to be loaded up and ready to move at first light, and told me where C was, now reunited. David was asleep, exhausted; he sat up, listened to the orders; asked a couple of questions, grunted and lay down and I followed suit when I had counted the noses of the sleeping platoon. Next morning we weren't ready to move at first light, for David had still been sound asleep while apparently listening to me. It was a mad scramble, and a very black mark for 2nd Lt. Cochrane, not fit to be trusted to transmit an order.

The objective that day was our old friend, Maktila Camp. We moved up to an attacking position, seeing no resemblance to what we thought the terrain to be like two months earlier in the dark, but it surrendered before we came to blows. That night we travelled south to attack two other camps, at Sofafi and Rabia, but were halted on the news that the garrisons had skipped. By then, Wavell was already implementing his decision to switch the 4th Indian Division to another theatre of war, maintaining the momentum of his desert victory with the 6th Australian Division; but our instructions on the morning of Thursday December 12th to return to our old position at Gerâwla didn't give any hint of that.

The journey there took four days because we were often halted while the transport was sent off to ferry prisoners back. The Italian airforce was much more in evidence, and we were dive-bombed and machine-gunned while we sat in our lorries in convoy. At least the planes were low enough to justify loosing off at them; it is demoralizing for an infantryman to be attacked by something he can see but which is too fast or too high to form a target.

Although I thought my lapse over passing on orders to the company would keep me in the doghouse, Tony Noble detailed me to take all the transport on to the Gerâwla position, unload the stores and return to pick up the battalion; every prospect, I feared, of losing the lot and probably my commission into the bargain. But the desert was now scored with tracks, mercifully in the right direction, and the only problem arose during a blinding dust storm, during which we had to cross the tarmac road running south from the coast to Siwa Oasis. Half the drivers went whizzing down the road, perhaps to prove that such a rarity wasn't just a mirage, and my flock took some rounding up once the storm had passed and visibility returned.

Several times on the trip to the old position and then back again to the battalion I needed something—water, petrol once for the convoy, or directions—and it was noticeable how one could call on any unit in the division, almost as though it were one's own. The divisional badge of the red eagle, or ruddy shite-hawk as the Jocks called it, was a passport that took one into any mess or cookhouse; we did best out of the exchange, since chapattis and dahl were a welcome change to us, while our rations were not in all cases acceptable to the Indian soldiers.

As well as a very effective fighting machine, the Indian Army was a remarkable social institution, not least in its ability to blend the two great and divisive religions of India within a single unit. Some regiments were recruited solely from one creed, such as the Gurkhas, but many contained two companies of Hindus or of Sikhs and two of Muslims, who soldiered together in complete amity and shared a fiercely possessive pride in the regiment. Mixed regiments were organized in companies of the same religion, purely because of rules over diet and cooking; even so, on active service the rules were cheerfully bent.

35

In Italy I once walked round the lines of the Frontier Force Regiment with their C.O., Dick Finch. Behind a stone wall we found a subadar with a pile of bully beef tins denuded of their labels: question and answer, and roars of laughter. The subsequent translation for my benefit ran like this:

'What on earth do you think you are doing, Subadar Sahib?'

'I'm doing something you can't do, Colonel, even though you command the battalion. I'm performing a miracle, turning beef into goat.'

Recruitment was very much a matter of selection from a crowd of applicants from a district or village where the regiment, or even one of its companies, had links. The recruit had to uphold the honour of his family and village, while striving to attach to himself the honour of the regiment, and the result was a very high standard of conduct. Men like this, with Indian officers and Viceroy-commissioned officers of long service, and British officers who spoke the language well and knew their men on and off parade, became superb soldiers.

I don't think it is imagination which makes me believe that Scots hit it off particularly well with Indian soldiers; the Jocks and the sepoys would certainly wander around in each other's lines when we were in rest, drinking each other's char, even if *Tik hai, Johnny?* was the extent of conversation. It may have been due to something of the same clannish regimental spirit. It was certainly helped by the fact that Indian battalions had pipe bands and enjoyed pipe music. The old tunes were given numbers for the Indian Army, so that *The Barren Rocks of Aden* or *The 79th's Farewell to Gibraltar* or *The Black Bear* became No. 4 or 37 or whatever, and it was usually necessary to whistle a few bars to get Scots and Indian pipers on the same wavelength.

My acquaintance with the Indian Army was almost entirely with the 4th Indian Division in which it was probably to be seen at its best, a division described by Wavell as 'one of the great fighting formations in military history: to be spoken of with such as The Tenth Legion, The Light Division of the Peninsular War, Napoleon's Old Guard'. The divisional spirit survived into the new and independent India. In the 1960's I met the then Indian military attaché at a reunion dinner; a Sikh officer, he had served with the 4th Indian in Italy in 1944, and we fell to talking about it and where it had fought. 'The worst time we had,' he remarked 'was up against the Chinese', and gravelled me. The Italians in Africa, the Germans in the desert and Tunisia, at Cassino and the Gothic Line — but when had we fought the Chinese? Then I realized that he was referring to the Chinese invasion of Tibet and India in 1950, when the division had been sent straight up into the snowy passes from the plains. For him, military history was a continuum, and the 4th Indian was the same formation that had so distinguished itself between 1940 and 1945.

* * *

We were filthy on our return, and 15 Platoon had grown a fine range of beards, the meagreness of my own masked by layer upon layer of dirt. To hell with the water ration; we cooked it by the gallon to provide baths of a sort and the luxury of a shave, and we felt no end of fine fellows. We had the sense to realize that we had been lucky enough to be involved in a walk-over, and that we had got off very lightly. Out of some 400 engaged, the battalion had only had 49 casualties, 7 of them officers, but when the dead or wounded had been friends the lightness of the casualties wasn't so apparent. In fact, it had been a great victory, though more of planning and logistics than of hard fighting. The threat to Eygpt had been a real one, and no one knew in advance how inept that particular Italian army was to prove. It had consisted, I was told

37

later by a scornful Italian regular soldier, of Blackshirt divisions and Libyan levies, in most cases poorly led and unwilling to fight. We were to learn soon how formidable an enemy good Italian troops could be.

3

SUDAN AND ERITREA

GERÂWLA and the Bagush Box didn't hold us for long, since almost at once we were told we would be going back to Alex to refit, and I was given four days' leave. Instead of having to sweat through a battalion move, I had three clear days of hot baths and clean clothes, most of which were David's, because my uniform had gone astray on the railway. I visited our wounded men in hospital; it happened to be the 15th General, with which I'd travelled out on the *Aquitania*, so the nurses were old friends. David's wife, Ethel, was in Cairo (several of the regimental wives had come on from India, instead of going home, and were working at GHQ); so I had the pleasure, resplendent in her husband's blue patrol and mess trews, of taking her out to dine and dance. I lunched with a friend in the Scots Guards mess at Kasr-el-Nil barracks, and a number of us went to the races at Gezira. It was a charming spectacle like a Dufy painting, though the normal hazards of betting were increased by the fact that nearly all of the jockeys had been warned off the pre-war turf of England, France and Australia.

On Christmas Eve I went back to Alex in luxury by car, shared with a fellow Cameron, Kenneth Milne. We found the battalion at Amriya, twenty miles from the city. It was a dismal site, but the company was revelling in sleeping with a roof over its head in the shape of bell tents. We celebrated Christmas by having dinner with our companies and by spending the evening in the Sergeants' Mess, whence a very thick head on Boxing Day. This was my first experience of a battalion mess, and therefore of living amongst all the officers instead of with the two or three in C Company. It was pleasant to meet off-parade the august figures of the Colonel and the Second-in-Command, Colin Duncan, and the commanders of the other companies whom I had previously seen only from a distance. Oddly, out of the thirty-odd months I was actually with the 2nd Battalion, I only spent three or four in a battalion mess; the rest of the time I was living with C Company.

We were reinforced with a big draft of Leicesters and Sherwood Foresters, forty-four of whom came to the company, very confused at being turned into instant Cameron Highlanders. In the midst of re-fitting with kit and equipment, it was not easy or very practicable to make them feel at home, or indeed to communicate at first, since broad Scots and the Midland vowels afforded very little common ground of comprehension. Some wag promptly called them the Free British and the nickname stuck; they were a useful lot of soldiers and NCOs, and were very soon an integrated part of the company—my first example of the remarkable powers of absorption by a good unit, the more striking because their original regiments have distinguished histories.

It wasn't all work, and there was time for high jinks in Alex, where the men were taken in buses. The Jocks ran wild, with plenty of unspent pay and the knowledge that we probably wouldn't see the fleshpots for a while. The redcaps and regimental police were busy popping drunks into lorries, for all the world like the scene at Waverley Station as the last train leaves for Swansea after a Welsh match at Murrayfield. Next day Wattie Reid marched the company by squads into David's Company Office for sentence; the more heinous offenders, who had been obstreperously drunk rather than quietly 'fou', were passed on to the Orderly Room where Andy was equally busy dishing out the punishments—all parties in the best of humours. The crime that evidently irked RSM Cameron most was that of a few cheerful souls, running round and round the waiting buses in Alex and shouting 'You canna' catch me, Gorgie, you canna' catch me': 'Gorgie', since the RSM came from that district of Edinburgh. This was a pretty obvious nickname, but there was real ingenuity in some of them. One senior officer always held his head at a slight angle, not unlike a pigeon, and was consequently known as either The Doo or Heid-the-Ba'. Inevitably you overheard your own nickname; mine took the innocuous form of Wee Pe'er, slightly galling since I was as tall as most of my platoon.

We paid for our fun with a dolorous Hogmanay sitting for seven hours by the railway line waiting for a train; the pipers did their best, but without a dram between us, it seemed a poor start to 1941.

On New Year's Day we embarked at Suez for the short trip down the Red Sea to Port Sudan. Entraining, detraining, embarking and disembarking, embussing and debussing are tedious when your responsibilities consist of soldiers, but when you are Baggage Officer and are responsible as a very junior officer for the whole battalion's kit and stores, those manœuvres are hideous. Anything unguarded was whipped at once, since there was a black market in Egypt for anything and everything. At least the potential thieves were recognizably civilians; the lot of the Baggage Officer was unhappier later in Italy, when other divisions, British or Allied, were always on the lookout for replenishments of kit. The army has a fondness for moving at night, however far from the firing line, and loading and unloading in the dark added another dimension to the game.

Years later, I had dinner with a Cameron Highlander who had been Baggage Officer when the battalion moved from India to Egypt in 1939: there was a strict limit on the size of personal kit, and the then C.O. owned a wooden box of colossal proportions, built to his own specification. The Baggage Officer got it on board, the ship's Transport Officer promptly put it off, and it lay on the quay while both parties informed him in ringing tones of a Baggage Officer's duty. I've forgotten what happened to the box, but he ended up, he claimed, by being put under arrest both by the Colonel and the Transport Officer.

Our ship was a very comfortable liner, and we all wished the voyage a longer one. The *Reina del Pacifico* had been on the South American run in peacetime, and it was inspiring to be, if only for a few days, a *Caballero* rather than a *Gent*. Apart from P.T. by companies, we weren't very military, and amused ourselves by dancing reels to the pipes and Tony Noble's 'squeezebox'—he played the accordion splendidly. January 6th saw us at Port Sudan; the baggage, apart from several things which got lost in the dark and confusion, was unloaded and reloaded into a train by 9.30 p.m. Our immediate destination was a railway junction called Haiya which consisted of two big water tanks and some tents. Our M.T. had been shipped separately at Alex and hadn't arrived, so the whole battalion's baggage had to be shifted in one borrowed lorry, trundling to and fro all day in a stinging sandstorm. It was a horrible day, and made me vow that I would never be caught for the job of Baggage Officer again, even if it meant feigning illness or lunacy: one of the few vows I've managed to keep.

We spent ten days here, mostly in training to blend the new draft with the old sweats. The country was lunar in its desolation, the foreground sand and flat black stones with occasional scrub, the background convulsed masses of bare rock rising to 3,000 and 4,000 feet. They looked not unlike the naked hills of Wester Ross, though with a very different temperature. Being winter, it was only in the 90's which after the bitter cold of the desert was very welcome, especially since we had the sybaritic water ration of six gallons a day, with showers at the station as a bonus. There was much more wild life than in the desert; on our route marches we saw hares, gazelle and ostriches.

Our next move was to a curious forest with a sandy floor, I suppose a wadi where enough water lay beneath the bed to let the trees flourish. Here it was enchanting to see the birds, brilliant little creatures flashing blue and yellow and green through the dense shade. I realized how much I had missed bird life in the desert. There was no leisure to watch them; we were making our final preparations and learning why we were in the Sudan, what we were going to do, and trying to make sense of the sketchy maps of the country ahead of us. Their inadequacy was compounded by the fact that they were printed on cotton, and thus far too convenient as sweat rags.

*   *   *

Eritrea, an Italian colony since the late nineteenth century, is a wedge of particularly mountainous and barren Africa, running inland from its port, Massawa, at the foot of the Red Sea, to Kassala on the Sudan frontier. The capital, Asmara, lies on a plateau between the two. In 1936, Eritrea was the base for the Italian invasion and conquest of Ethiopia, its neighbour to the south, and nearly ten times larger; with Italian Somaliland, the whole area formed Italy's East African empire, Africa Orientale. It was an uneasy empire, for although Eritrea was settled by many Italians and contributed excellent soldiers to the army, Ethiopia was barely subjugated, and required a large standing army scattered about in strong-points to hold down the people.

The conquerors of Eritrea built a railway from Massawa up country, as was de rigeur for all colonial powers. In the thirties no more railways were built to open up Ethiopia; instead the Italians, who must be the finest road engineers in the world, had built some superb highways across very difficult terrain, and used fleets of heavy lorries. Ethiopia at least produced food, but oil and petrol, industrial goods and armaments, settlers and soldiers all had to come through the Suez Canal. With the approach of war, a certain amount of stockpiling had been done, but it was clear that the British hold on Suez, unless broken by Graziani's invasion of Egypt, would eventually strangle Italian East Africa.

The Duke of Aosta, governor general and C. in C., had conflicting advice from those who felt that any forward policy would lose Ethiopia and those who argued that a thrust into the Sudan and the capture of Khartoum would force Wavell to counter with half the forces in Egypt and leave Graziani with an easy task. In the event, just as in Libya, a half-hearted incursion was made over the frontier, and then allowed to stagnate while the British riposte was prepared. This was the more surprising in that the Italians had overrun British Somaliland with ease in August 1940.

Major General Platt commanded the Sudan Defence Force and had in addition one British brigade to cover a frontier of some 1,200 miles. The S.D.F. were turned into moss troopers in a new border warfare; their vigorous patrolling, always offensive, and their incessant switches from one area to another convinced the Italians that Platt, or the Kaid to give him his Sudanese title, disposed of far bigger forces than the handful he had. Substance was given to enemy intelligence reports by the arrival from India of the 5th Indian Division, by which time Aosta had missed his opportunity; the addition of the 4th Indian from Egypt meant that the British could take the offensive from the Sudan, to coincide with an advance from Kenya into southern Ethiopia and with the return of Emperor Haile Selassie to his kingdom.* It was psychologically important for Britain that the Emperor should be restored, which entailed knocking out the 300,000 strong Italian army in Eritrea and Ethiopia. In addition, it was the only way to make sure that Massawa did not remain a potential enemy submarine base on the Red Sea.

There were two routes from the Sudan into Eritrea, through Kassala which had been occupied by the Italians;

* An excellent account of the campaign as a whole is given by A. J. Barker, *Eritrea 1941* (Faber 1966).

the northern followed the main road, laid down as our route, while the southern was to be forced by the 5th Indian. The 4th Indian had now been made up to its full strength of three brigades, but the 7th Brigade had been left to defend Port Sudan which was easily accessible from northern Eritrea; so we consisted of the 5th Indian Infantry Brigade (1st Royal Fusiliers, 3rd/1st Punjab Regiment, 4th (Outram's)/6th Rajputana Rifles) and the 11th (2nd Cameron Highlanders, 3rd/14th Punjab Regiment who replaced the Rajputs, and 1st (Wellesley's)/6th Rajputana Rifles). Our gunners were the 1st, 25th and 31st Field Regiments R.A., our recce or armoured unit the Central India Horse. Apart from the artillery and the British battalion in each brigade, it was an Indian division in fact as well as name; the engineers were units of The Bengal, The Madras and The Royal Bombay Sappers and Miners, and transport, signal and medical units were all Indian Army.

We hadn't in the desert seen much at close quarters of our fellow battalions in the brigade, but we had worked closely enough to know that our operations were well planned and co-ordinated. And when at company and platoon level soldiers feel that the command knows what it is doing, and has a staff capable of getting the right part of the jigsaw to the right place at the right time, whether that is artillery support, or a flanking battalion, or just the rations, morale is always high. Also we knew our brigadier, who visited his units often; Reggie Savory was a stocky little man with an enormous and pugnacious chin, as good at chatting up the Jocks as he was in talking to the sepoys.

We were therefore bursting with confidence when we had our orders to capture Kassala as a prelude to invading Eritrea; even more so when we learnt that the garrison had slipped away. We dumped most of our kit (promptly looted) and piled into trucks, following in the wake of Gazelle Force, a mixed group of motorized S.D.F.

and Sikhs and Skinner's Horse. Gazelle pursued with
great verve until they were halted in the Keru gorge, the
hills either side held in strength and the road mined; the
Sikhs immediately swarmed up one of the ridges but were
checked, with over 150 casualties. It was now our turn;
all the battalion had suffered so far was a few casualties in
A Company, on the road to Keru, from anti-personnel
grenades dropped by five Savoia bombers. They lumbered
round so low and so slowly that everybody had a shot at
them, even those whose only weapon was a pistol, but to
no discernible effect.

C Company was little changed since the desert, except
for the commander. David had been transferred to
command A Company, being replaced by Major Crispe-
Clarke. Jackie was a Somerset Light Infantryman, seconded
to the Camerons because we were short of officers, and
conspicuous in a sea of balmorals with his dark side-cap.
As the only other officer in the company, I was second-in-
command, which in effect meant commanding 15 Platoon
while being available for any administrative jobs: with
veterans as sergeant-major and quartermaster sergeant,
the admin looked after itself. The only change in the
platoon was the addition of half a dozen men from the
draft and the fact that the burly Patterson now lugged
poor Crowe's anti-tank rifle.

At least that bit of lumber could be left behind when we
were ordered up the hill to relieve the Sikhs; the rest
of the battalion organized themselves for an attack that
night. It was our first taste of climbing after spending so
long on the flat, and we were puffed even though it was a
little hill compared with those we met later; a counter-
attack would have been awkward. The lean men got up
in better order, despite the weight of weapons, ammunition
and water bottle, than the big oxes, 'the busty yins'. We
found, as so often is the case, that the 'top' where the
Sikhs were in position was a false crest, the Italians still
holding the true summit. All that happened was an

exchange of rifle and light machine-gun fire, with no casualties to us.

Keru was the scene of a gallant action that passed into the division's mythology, the exploit of 'the man on the white horse' who twice led charges of his Eritrean cavalry on our gun positions, to help cover the withdrawal of the Italian infantry. This must be the last instance of a cavalry charge in war, and was very nearly successful, since only at the last moment did the gunners, firing over open sights, drive them off. Long after the war we learned that the officer in command of the cavalry, Baron Amedeo Guillet, had survived. He led a guerilla force after Eritrea had been over-run; when he was smoked out, he managed to cross the Red Sea disguised as an Arab and found sanctuary in the Yemen, whence he somehow made his way back to Italy. After the war his distinguished career as a diplomat included the post of Italian ambassador in Delhi. He happened to be in London in 1976 and, thanks to Reggie Savory's initiative, he dined with the old officers of the division. It was a memorable and rather emotional occasion, and a great pleasure for us all to meet again, in happier circumstances than that campaign, so courageous an opponent.

Thanks in part to his action, the enemy rearguard at Keru withdrew overnight in good order. Once the mines had been cleared, together with the iron-spiked rail sleepers scattered along the road, Gazelle Force went pounding off again. We followed, but this time on foot; our complete transport had still not caught us up. It was very hot indeed, and sixteen miles proved a long march; we did another fourteen next day, and ten men in the company, nearly all from the Free British draft, collapsed with heat stroke. Discipline comes into its own when a soldier has to make his water bottle last all day, while his tongue is swelling and there is no spittle to swallow. It helped to suck a pebble, though it was liable to burn the mouth. I ended up carrying a couple of rifles, and couldn't decide whether one did that sort of thing because it was expected (conformism is another aspect of not letting the side down) or through sheer vanity; either way, I regretted it. At the day's end, there was the battalion water truck which had been sent ahead to our halting place, and there, blessed sight, were the company cooks with dixies full of boiling hot sweet char.

The third day, Sunday January 26th, it was our turn for M.T., to leapfrog us forward to the outskirts of Agordat, a provincial town ringed with hills which the enemy had prepared as the position for a major stand. We spent until Friday 31st taking up one position after another, edging

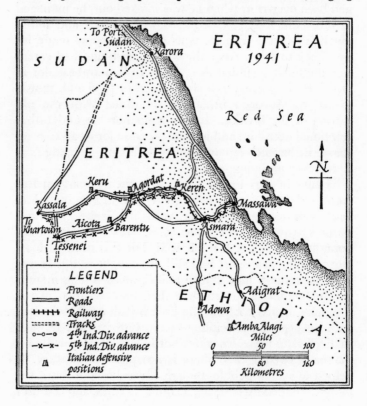

round the defences while the divisional attack was prepared. The southern approach to the town was guarded by a long ridge, Laquetat; to its east lay a plain about two miles across, and then a very big lump of a hill, Mount Cochen. Both Laquetat and Cochen, which was the brigade objective, were pitted with well-sited emplacements and trenches, and held in strength. Beyond Cochen lay the main road to Asmara, the Via Imperiale; if we could cut that, we would have the garrison boxed up. Even to threaten it would lead to a withdrawal, since the Italians had proved sensitive to any outflanking movement.

The Punjabis assaulted Cochen and had a very rough time, scrambling up the steep slopes, round the cottage-sized boulders, encountering heavy fire and showers of grenades, and being counter-attacked off ground that they had won. A problem in all these Eritrean battles was the scale of the landscape: a battalion committed to those huge hills soon became a scattered mass of sections, with everything hingeing on the drive and determination of the individual soldier and the junior leader. To make the brigadier or commanding officer's task worse, he had to deploy a sizeable proportion of his force in carrying ammunition and water up to the attacking troops. While we were battering at Cochen, 5th Brigade were having no more success at Laquetat; each hill gave excellent observation on the forces attacking the other, and the Italians handled their artillery well.

Cochen had a foothill sticking out into the plain towards Laquetat; we called it Gibraltar. The Camerons were ordered to take it, to give a little leverage on the flank of Cochen. Two companies assaulted it, while C Company was ordered to clear the plain round its base; we were then to exploit to the main road. Unlike Sidi Barrani, there was no doubt about where our objective was. We set off in open order, because the fire down onto the plain was fierce. Jackie was hit almost at once, so I found myself in command; at least on the flat it was possible to see most of the company which made control easier, and led me to carry on with 15 Platoon. We pushed round the base of Gibraltar, and then along the edge of Cochen itself, where the shooting was even more intense. Luckily, plunging fire is less lethal than level shooting, but Sgt. Horbury was killed fairly early, with another four men, and sixteen men were wounded, including all three of my section commanders in 15 Platoon, McGregor, Hawley and Patterson, promoted from his anti-tank rifle to Lance-Corporal. It was the mark of well-trained professional soldiers that the platoon still functioned as a unit and carried on with its job without a sergeant and with the oldest soldier in each section taking over its command without any orders being required.

We met little opposition on the ground, but did have a fright from a medium tank which appeared suddenly with its lid open and commander peering out. By this time we were rather too scattered to be effective, and God knows where that infernal anti-tank rifle was; equally, I suppose we offered a poor target. The lid shut with a clang and the tank retired, circling a tree one way while I circled nervously the other. By now, the companies were established on Gibraltar and could see tanks and a battalion forming up for a counter-attack over the plain. Three of our own tanks, of the seven available for the campaign, were up near battalion HQ; Colin Duncan jumped into one and led them round the corner where their two-pounders killed the thinly-armoured Italian tanks and dispersed the battalion. The capture of Gibraltar coincided with a new and successful attack on Cochen by every man the brigadier could find; and in turn the enemy began streaming up the road away from Agordat.

That was a sad night; the whole company was downcast by Horbury's death, far more so than by the total number of casualties, and I felt it keenly. He had been an unfailing prop, and a good friend in all my raw inexperience. But the army doesn't give much time for the luxury

of grief, and none at all after an action. The company had
to be re-arranged to fill the gaps, reports made to battalion
HQ, and everything readied up for the next move.

On Wattie Reid's excellent advice, I moved Corporal
Ramage from 14 Platoon to fill the vacancy as platoon
sergeant in 15. A dark, saturnine man, he made a good
sergeant, though for me he could never replace Horbury.
Alan George Cameron—the double Christian name to
distinguish him from the other Alan Cameron—was sent
across from A Company to take over command of C, to
my relief and pleasure. He was an ex-Scots Guardsman, a
tough soldier and an amusing companion. C Company
was now in the unusual position of being officered solely
by two second lieutenants; but Alan George was an
exceptionally experienced soldier to be a subaltern, and
commanded the company with skill and gusto.

No fighting for us next day, which was just as well.
Instead, the company was pushed four kilometres up the
road to guard dumps of Italian ammunition and rations,
which included a whole lorryload of delicious tinned
tomatoes and another of vermouth. The main prize, however, though we didn't realize its value till later, was a
complete mule train. We drove off the native looters and
then turned to animal husbandry. The Jocks thought this
was a real lark, and they off-saddled the mules and fed and
watered them as though they'd been muleteers all their
service. All this activity stopped any moping, and was
good for us all, as well as for the mules.

Meanwhile Gazelle Force had been chasing up the road
after the retreating enemy: Frank Messervy who led it had
only one command for his Sudanese and Indians, 'Bum
on, regardless.' We followed in M.T., covering about
40 miles, but with a hold up at a magnificent bridge
which had been blown. The dry riverbed beneath it had
been mined, and it took eight hours dangerous work by the
Sappers and Miners before Gazelle Force and the brigade
could get on. It is arguable that, without that delay, we

might have forced Keren before the enemy could hold it in strength, and thus avoided 3,000 casualties. More important, if there had not been a seven-week battle at Keren, Wavell would have had the 4th Indian Division back in the desert two months before he did, with incalculable consequences on Rommel's first assault.

Luckily, we had nobody in the company cursed with the second sight, and when we finally moved again, we went whizzing along the splendid road wondering if we'd have any more hitches before Asmara. We could hear Gazelle firing and being fired on, and a bend brought us in sight of the trouble. The Via Imperiale here traversed a valley floor, ringed with hills like an amphitheatre, with the railway line running in parallel along the lower slopes of the northern range. The road disappeared in a narrow gorge cutting through the ring of peaks, and the shining thread of the railway stopped at the black entrance of a tunnel. The Italians had blown about a hundred yards of the road into the gorge, and then for good measure blown half a hillside on top of where the road used to be. It was a complete block; and unlike the blown bridge, it was defended. Just beyond the road block and the ring of mountains lay the small town of Cheren, as it was shown on our very inadequate handkerchief maps, or Keren as it was officially spelt later.

KEREN: Brig's Peak (*left*) and Sanchil (*right*) from the valley floor. The cross was marked on the photo to show Kenneth Milne's parents where his body was found

KEREN: Indian Sappers making a track

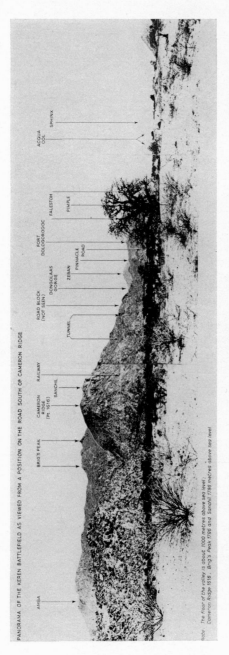

PANORAMA OF THE KEREN BATTLEFIELD AS VIEWED FROM A POSITION ON THE ROAD SOUTH OF CAMERON RIDGE

AMBA

BRIG'S PEAK

CAMERON RIDGE (Pt. 1616)

SANCHIL

RAILWAY

ROAD BLOCK (NOT SEEN)

TUNNEL

DONGOLAAS GORGE

ZEBAN

PINNACLE ROAD

FORT DOLOGORODOC

PIMPLE

FALESTOH

ACQUA COL

SPHINX

Note: The floor of the valley is about 1000 metres above sea level:
Cameron Ridge 1616. Brig's Peak 1795 and Sanchil 1796 metres above sea level

KEREN: Panorama of the Keren battlefield from a position south of Cameron Ridge

4

KEREN

MOUNTAIN warfare is like fishing a strange loch. There is a daunting expanse of water, and one's flies look very insignificant. But one must start somewhere if trout are to be caught, and a blend of guesswork and experience tells one where to begin. In this case, the peaks were as fearsome to the left as to the right of the blocked pass, but on the left there was a partly detached hill, pierced by the tunnel into which the railway line disappeared. This, it was thought, would at least give some observation for our guns onto a fort crowning one of the lower hills to the right. That was where to begin, and C Company was the first cast.

We plodded on for a mile or so over the flat valley floor with hardly a shell to disturb our march, but in full view of any spectators in the surrounding stadium. Our destination must have been unmistakeable. We drew a deep breath at the foot of the hill and began climbing, 14 and 15 Platoons leading. The going was difficult with big boulders to dodge round and a lot of loose stones underfoot, on a very steep gradient. Each section had to pick its own route, with occasional bawling from me to move more right or left. I was only guessing, for the hill was a stiff one, the crest nearly 2,000 feet above the valley, and too steep to give one any view of the top. It was simpler when the shooting began and helpfully provided an immediate objective, if we wanted to stop being the target.

There was about a company of the enemy on the ridge. I fancy they had arrived not long before we did, with time only to scratch out a few positions for their light machine guns and bomb-throwers above the railway line and on

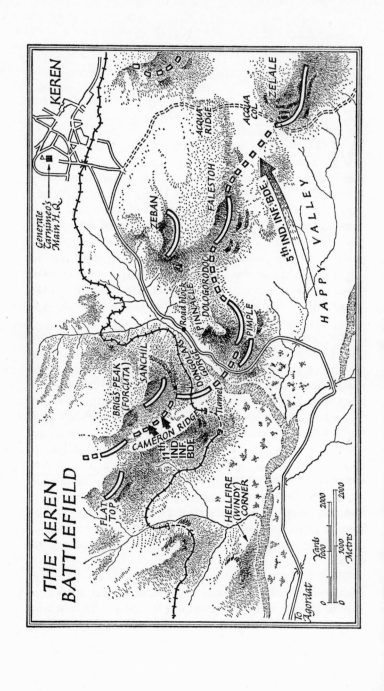

THE KEREN BATTLEFIELD

KEREN

Generale
Carnimeo's
Main H.Q.

ZEBAN

ACQUA
RIDGE

FALESTOH

ACQUA
COL

ZEBAN

ZELALE

DOLOGORODOC

Road Line
PINNACLE

PIMPLE

5ᵗʰ IND. INF. BDE.

BRIG'S PEAK
(FORCUTA)

SANCHIL

DONGOLAC
GORGE

Tunnel

CAMERON RIDGE

11ᵗʰ
IND.
INF. BDE.

HAPPY VALLEY

FLAT
TOP

HELLFIRE
(WINDY)
CORNER

To
Agordat

Yards
1000   2000

0   1000   2000
Metres

the bump over the tunnel. The only way to get on terms
was to reach their level. It had been an hour's hard work
to climb the 1,000 feet to the railway, and a breather
would have been welcome; but there is nothing like being
shot at to generate extra agility. PSM Galloway was hit
as we reached the railway line; he was a big, heavy man
and so badly blown by the climb that he probably would
not have been an effective commander for some time, so
there was nothing lost by my having to bellow orders to
14 Platoon as well as 15.

There were odd parties of Italians here and there, but
the main defence consisted of two light machine-gun
positions, well sited to give cross-fire. One of them was
overlooked by a crag, and it looked as though it would be
simple to lob grenades into it if one could perch on top.
I told Ramage to keep shooting, while I ran and crawled
(painfully, with bare knees) until the foot of the crag
gave cover from the second machine gun. I clambered up
and pulled some Mills bombs from my haversack, pitching
them down with real malice, for the machine-gunner had
located me again. Unfortunately there was an overhang
of rock off which my grenades bounced harmlessly. I
could see Corporal Watson of 14 Platoon and, more
important, he could decipher my hand signals. He
brought his section under cover of some thorn bushes to
the firing position indicated, gave a copy-book five order
— 'See yon big yellow stane—nine o'clock—enemy in
sangar—fifty yards, five rounds—Fire!'—and hit eight
of the nine men in it.

We then had to climb fast again to knock out the
second gun, over the tunnel. The hillside was more open
here, giving us as well as the enemy a field of fire, so one
section of 15 Platoon could occupy the Italians with bren
gun fire while the other two skipped like goats from boulder
to boulder. We leapfrogged like this until we were close
enough for a final rush, preceded by a couple of grenades.
I was in a berserk state of rage at the machine-gunner

because he had frightened me so badly, and he was the first man I killed in the hand to hand scramble as we jumped over the breastwork. Our attack left fourteen enemy dead, with four prisoners.

Alan George and the rest of the company were up at the railway, and his signaller just had time to heliograph our news to battalion HQ down in the valley before the sun slid behind the peaks. Our casualties had been very few, but to try to consolidate our position on such a massive feature was like scattering a pinch of lettuce seed over a rockery, a fact realized by Andy who soon pushed D Company up, as well as water and ammunition. Eventually the hill, christened Cameron Ridge by the division, was to be occupied by two battalions, with plenty of room for the full brigade when attacks were launched from it.

In the failing light we could see how completely our Ridge was overlooked by the further peaks of Mt. Sanchil and its neighbours. Between lay a shallow ravine across which the inevitable counter-attack would come. I stayed with 15 in the tunnel area, putting two sections up on the bump on top, while Alan George deployed the rest of the company to the left. The platoon was in great fettle, though we were very tired and desperate for a mug of char; however, thanks to good water discipline, every man still had half a water bottle full. The Jocks were delighted that the little fire and movement operation had come off so neatly; it was encouraging to find that training produced positive results. One of the sections had been led with great dash by our old incorrigible, 37 Smith, still a private. At some point one of the men in it had become separated, very easy on that hillside, and had shouted 'Smithy! Smithy! Where are you?' The answering shout from Smith was 'In the f—— enemy post where you should f—— be.'

As the war went on, I grew interested in the psychology of attack and defence. However strong the defences or forlorn a hope the assault may look, the attack has the initiative and the psychological advantage, but only as long as the momentum is kept going. When it falters, the defence realizes that the attack may fail, the advantage passes and the attack almost certainly will fail. There is no problem when the assault is a ram-stam affair of a single rush, but nearly every attack involves some sort of re-grouping or change of line, even down to the lowly level of the platoon. With seasoned troops, this can be done without loss of momentum, even if at the moment no one is actually moving forward, but when the soldiers or their junior leaders are inexperienced and bewildered the pause to re-group can be fatal to success. This is not just due to the fact that if one goes to ground under fire, it requires a real effort of will to stand up again; it is also because in all the noise and danger of action one is inclined to think the worst. Any pause therefore can be taken by raw troops as a sign that the attack has already failed, where old sweats will sit tight until the next command reaches them.

We had two alarms that night. The first was a series of three attacks on the sections up on the bump, all of which came to nothing; the second was in the tunnel itself. From the bump one couldn't see down to the tunnel mouth on the enemy side of the hill, and I didn't fancy taking a patrol through it because we would have been too easy a target emerging at the other end. Instead, I fixed up a bren gun just inside the mouth on our side. After the three counter-attacks had been beaten off I took a nap from which Sgt. Ramage woke me with the news that the sentry could hear voices and movement inside the tunnel. I told the gunner, happy man, to let fly, which produced a staggering noise, the bursts of auto-matic fire magnified a hundred times in the tunnel. But it was nothing to the noise a few minutes later—a colossal, rending crash followed by a choking cloud of dust which billowed out of the entrance. The Italians had blocked the rails in some way and then let slip down the incline into the tunnel several wagons loaded with rock. The smash-up shut the tunnel as effectively as their man-made landslide had blocked the road. I realized a bit late in the day that the fairly noisy attacks on the bump had probably been diversions to cover the preparation of this stroke.

Next morning we looked with growing respect at the immense natural strength of the Italian position. We looked upward, for the ring of peaks commanded our hill, except for the view from the bump down on the road block in the gorge. The Italians were still working on our side of the great landslide, presumably laying mines. Before we opened up with the brens, I wanted a shot myself, my excuse being that I needed to establish the range since it was a dropping shot and the brilliant mountain light was misleadingly clear. I am still ashamed of the inordinate pleasure I felt at hitting my man with a single round, 1,000 yards on the sight. Like the man doing a hole in one in his first game of golf, I could now give up shooting as far as 15 Platoon was concerned.

D Company was now up on the Ridge and Major Neilson took command of both companies. Robbie Neilson had come to the Camerons on accelerated promotion from the Gordons, a genial man who went to some trouble to be kindly to junior officers in other companies, so he was no stranger. However affable off parade, he had a voice like ripping calico when he issued orders. Under him we had to hold the Ridge while the Punjabis went through to attack Mt. Sanchil's nearest neighbour, subsequently known as Brig's Peak, over 5,000 feet. By the time one got to the floor of the ravine in front of Cameron Ridge, it was about a 2,000 foot climb to the summit of Brig's Peak or Sanchil. It was a recurring feature of this horrible battle that not enough troops were able to reach the objective to hold it against counter-attack. The Punjabis with great verve seized Brig's Peak, and indeed next morning could look down on the town of Keren beyond the ring of hills that protected it, but a ferocious counter-attack by the Savoy Grenadiers drove them off with heavy losses and for a time looked like re-taking Cameron Ridge as well, with D Company bearing the brunt of the fighting. By nightfall we were reinforced by the 1st/6th Rajputana Rifles who took over the left of the Ridge, and for the next ten days the Raj Rif and Camerons held on grimly, forging in the process a bond of mutual affection and respect. This found expression in a pipe tune, and a good tune too, *With Wellesley's Rifles at Keren*, composed by Corporal Kearney and officially presented to the 1st/6th during an interval in the desert fighting later that year.

It was learned later that the Italians' original plan had been to fall right back after Agordat to a position covering Asmara, and that they had only belatedly recognized the enormous strength of the Keren position. It had been a race to get men up on the summits, which the Italians won, committing fresh troops rushed from Ethiopia and northern Eritrea. These, as I was told by them proudly later, were units of the Royal Army, unlike the Black-shirt divisions we had over-run in the desert, and they fought as bravely and skilfully as men can. They consisted of units of the Savoy Grenadiers, Bersaglieri and Alpini with colonial battalions of Eritreans, excellent soldiers as long as they were well led. The enemy artillery that bothered us most was not their scanty medium guns but the pack batteries, which scrambled up into almost impossible positions to lob shells onto us, and the heavy mortars, handled with great skill and severe effect. In comparison the otherwise superb 25-pounders of our field regiments had a fairly flat trajectory and couldn't search the rear slopes near the top of these steep hills.

All we knew at the time was that Sanchil and Brig's Peak were strongly held, and that Cameron Ridge was a precarious position since, apart from counter-attacks, day-light movement among the forward sections immediately attracted sniper fire, while day and night at irregular intervals shells and mortar bombs crashed down all over it, their effect magnified by the rocky ground. However, we were clearly going to be there for some time. Making the best of it consisted of improving the positions; digging was almost impossible, so we built sangars for protection. No question of neatness now, speed was essential. It meant crawling about in daylight to decide where a field of fire best combined with adequate protection, and then constructing them after dark. In most cases it was possible to use outcrops of rock to reduce the labour of humping up flat stones for the walls, so our sangars looked like house martins' nests plastered onto the hillside.

By now the whole battalion was up on the Ridge and Andy got us organized with three companies up in the forward positions while the fourth served as carriers. The Sappers and Miners worked furiously to make a track of sorts from the valley floor to the railway line, and up this came the mules we had captured at Agordat with the precious water; ammunition and rations were still carried by hand until more mules arrived from Cyprus. From the railway, the mule track continued up the hill towards the Raj Rif on the left, but our position was on ground too steep for mules, so everything had to be man-handled.

Companies were rotated, but since C had not been counter-attacked since our first night we were left over the tunnel for several days with nothing but odd shelling and mortaring to keep us on our toes. We had some casualties, among them Pte. Roy, badly wounded in the head and stomach. He couldn't see, but gripped my hand when I got to him, begging me to finish him off with my pistol. I thought about it for an instant, because he was very smashed up; but the fluency of his cursing, when I told him I wouldn't, convinced me I was right — a conviction reinforced months later when we met in the cinema queue at a South African hospital. He was on sticks, and his face was the surgeon's art, not nature's; but he was chipper, and seemed glad I hadn't shot him.

Casualties were a problem. From the forward positions they could only be evacuated after dark, which meant keeping wounded men in the sections long after the initial anaesthetic of shock had worn off. We did our best for them, while they in turn tried to bottle up their groans as the pain of their wounds bit deep. Carrying a stretcher down the hill at night was worse than carrying rations and ammunition up it. For the wounded man, it must have been torment. Once down to the valley, there were ambulances to jolt from bump to bump until the road could be reached. To do so, all transport had to get round a foothill spur in full view and range of the enemy gunners; it was naturally called Hellfire Corner. The technique was either to go very fast or very slow, since normal pace meant precisely coinciding with a salvo. The ambulances moved at night whenever possible, which didn't lead to a smooth ride for the wounded.

On the night of February 6th there were very heavy attacks on the Raj Rif and on the left hand company of the Camerons, but no ground was lost. On the extreme right, C Company were spectators, as always in those circumstances with mixed feelings; relief that the enemy hadn't picked on us, anxiety lest an attack on our own position should develop, worry about how the others in the thick of it were getting on and concern that we couldn't do a thing to help. The following night began our opportunity to learn the topography of the rest of the Ridge, for we were relieved by B Company and spent three days on carrying. It was punishing work, since it was a two-hour climb to the forward companies, with the water in two-gallon tins, the ammunition and rations (bully beef and biscuit, tea, sugar and condensed milk) in sandbags. The utmost possible was two trips a day, and even that provided only a pint of water a day per man. This was little enough in the blazing heat of day; carrying at least kept one sweating at night, when it was very cold up on the top. Blankets or greatcoats couldn't possibly be carried up.

As one stumbled up the hill with one's load, the occasional mortar bomb or shell would drop; we swore more viciously at them than when we were stuck in the forward positions. One of the paths was covered by a fixed-line machine gun at night at a point where it was impossible to diverge, and uncertainty over whether the man at the other end was alert or nodding led to some swearing too. Someone who had read about the Siege of Sydney Street christened the unknown machine-gunner Peter the Painter, and the absurd nickname was taken up by the whole battalion.

Beside the track from the railway line down to the valley was a very dead mule, stinking if anything worse than the dead men, and hourly swelling to a vaster bulk. The brigadier rightly decreed that it must go, and since a mule is clearly transport, the job fell to the Brigade Transport Officer. He poured petrol over it, put a match to it, and was quite badly burnt in the resulting explosion, giving us one of our only wholehearted laughs for a fortnight.

When our stint of carrying was over, C Company went up to the crest again, this time in the centre of the line instead of our old area over the tunnel. After we had been up on top for a few days, Andy himself got hold of me on the field telephone: 'Peter, how about a change of air at battalion HQ for a couple of days?' This was thoughtful of him, even more thoughtful not to make it an order, because it would have been intolerable, as I am sure he knew, to have a rest while the company was still in the forward position.

While the 11th Brigade were sitting tight on Cameron Ridge, the 5th Brigade tried to penetrate the hills on the right of the gorge and the blocked road, but again the size of the features in relation to the forces available defeated the attempt. So we tried once more on our side, the 3rd/1st Punjabis, who had replaced the 3rd/14th, assaulting yet again Brig's Peak, with no more success. It was at this point that General Platt decided that there was no alternative to using both his divisions, accepting the delay involved in dumping enough stores forward to maintain such a force. As a result, brigade reliefs were possible, and on the night of the 15th–16th we were relieved by the Royal Fusiliers of the 5th Brigade, and thankfully clambered down the hill.

We had had about twenty-five casualties in the company, some only sick and therefore likely to rejoin soon; and C had done well. Some of the Free British were a bit frayed at the edges, but the professionalism of the old soldiers had steadied them. Several of the latter were made up to Lance-Corporal: Delaney, Pattinson, Laidlaw, Moir and Matthews. The last must have been a problem in peacetime, being the sort of soldier who on parade always seems to have half his chin unshaved and some vital buttons not merely undone but missing: however, he was imperturbable, and almost maddeningly cheerful.

One of the most frightening experiences in that fortnight was being shelled by our own artillery, three times when C Company was on top of the Ridge. It can happen easily enough in mountain country—we suffered in the same way at Cassino three years later—as the Forward Observation Officer, or F.O.O., endeavours to bring his guns down and down on the forward slopes facing him; sooner or later they will start clipping the top of his own feature, which he may not immediately notice if, as is usual, his observation post is to the flank of the line of fire and his guns are covering a wide arc. For the infantry it is far more unnerving than being bombed by your own planes, although that never happened to us in Eritrea. When the boys in blue have decanted their load they go away, and with luck the next lot's error will occur over someone else, perhaps even the enemy. To be shot up the back passage by your own guns when your rickety breast work is designed to give you protection from the front creates a paralysing terror.

The gunners are always convinced that the infantry cannot tell which direction a shell has come from, and since enemy shelling was often heavy and prolonged, they had a case for pooh-poohing cries of alarm. But on the second occasion we had two men killed, one wounded and three men temporarily reduced to idiocy, and so violent was my outrage on the telephone to battalion HQ that a battery commander came up to convince us that the shells were coming thataway, not thisaway. God be thanked, it happened again when he was with us; I've never seen a man jump so fast to grab a telephone.

These episodes apart, we thought the world of our gunners. The field regiments were very much an integral part of the division and gave us much more than fire support, since well-handled guns are a great fillip to morale. The liaison was close, thanks to the energy of the F.O.O.s up with the front line troops, directing shoots and calling down fire as required. During the Keren battle, no fewer than nineteen F.O.O.s were killed or wounded.

We suffered very little enemy bombing, thanks to the R.A.F. Despite their ancient machines, they succeeded at the outset of the campaign in destroying much of the Italian airforce on the ground.

When we climbed down from Cameron Ridge, our first night's march up the valley took us to an area searched by the enemy's medium guns, so we moved back another three kilometres, licked our wounds and cleaned up. We were very filthy, dust and dirt caked in layers, so the first joy was unlimited water. Even a famine of razor-blades didn't diminish the pleasure of scraping off our beards; we cleaned our teeth, a strange sensation; and every bush was festooned with shorts and shirts drying in the sun. We got some new boots to replace those worst cut about by the stony slopes; we got some mail; above all, after a long drive with two three-tonners, Toby Irvine appeared with gallons of beer and most of brigade HQ's allocation of whisky. C Company sat about in small groups, in our clean skins inside clean shirts, singing cheerfully round little fires and making the beer last as long as possible.

I did not care to let my fancy dwell too much on the previous fortnight or on the fact that we were clearly going back again. What we had seen and done had to be taken as part of the day's work, and as far as possible put out of mind. I was neither pleased nor ashamed at having killed a number of men, merely thankful that I had done so before they killed us; it was the memory of our own dead and wounded that had to be repressed. Nobody in 15 Platoon, I would say, was bloodthirsty in the sense of taking pleasure in maiming or killing fellow men, though we did it methodically enough; the kick came from success in achieving the object, not in the corpses we had made in the process. (Unlike watching synthetic violence on television, in real life the other man is doing his level best to kill you, which takes all the vicarious fun out of it.)

After a couple of days tidying up ourselves and our equipment, the CSM decided it was time for a parade or two. A patch of ground in our bivouac area was reasonably level and here the company went through its paces with arms drill and the limited amount of foot drill possible. Absurd? Far from it, it was an excellent stroke to have the company moving as a homogeneous unit again. Alan George Cameron and Wattie measured the prescription very carefully; too much would have been a bore for all ranks, but the right dose was a tonic. The Jocks put brio into their drill; it was a nice touch of 'Wha's like us?' and correspondingly good for morale. We were visited often by Andy, and also by the brigadier on our first washing day; he showed a startled admiration for a very complete fox hunt tattooed from top to bottom of a naked soldier's back.

After ten days' rest, we went back up the hill on the

night of February 26th–27th to our old positions on the Ridge, relieving the Fusiliers until in turn they relieved us on March 6th–7th. We followed the old routine of three companies up, one carrying, with a change-over every three days. There were no counter-attacks by the Italians, but fairly active patrolling at night and the usual shelling and mortaring by day and night. Within minutes of starting the climb from the valley, one seemed to be as dirty as ever. The Ridge had been no posy when we left it, although we had been rigid over refuse and had done our best (a poor one in those rocks) over latrine discipline; but when we got back there seemed to be empty tins and shit everywhere.

The corpses of course had been smelling to heaven since the second day of the battle; we tried to bury our dead, but explosions dug them up again, while the Italian and Indian and British bodies in the ravine in front of the Ridge just lay there, swelling.

There was a point in this process when a corpse had passed the stage of looking ludicrous or pathetic and reached that of the grotesque—when the normally loose uniform of shirt and shorts was filled to bursting point, every seam strained, by the tumid body inside, the skin shining as it was stretched tighter and tighter. When you come to think about it, and there was time enough to do that, there is a large number of familiar quotations in which 'flesh' is prominent, and I could remember too many of them.

To a point, we got used to the heavy, sweetish carrion smell of the dead since it was never out of our nose and lungs; the smell of human dung as well made us indignant. 'It spoils wer dinner,' complained Matthews, who had the wisdom not to think too much of the provenance of the flies paddling in the melted fat which constituted his bully beef. For the flies were there, it seemed in millions. The energetic, lively ones were a nuisance, but the sluggish, bloated crawlers were a horror.

66

Tobacco was a help. At least it irritated the flies when one puffed at them, while cigarette smoke inhaled to the very bottom of one's lungs over-rode for a moment or two the heavy smell of the dead. Pipe tobacco was very scarce, though an occasional lump of plug came my way; one needed a sharp knife and a leathery thumb to slice off little bits to fill a pipe. Then cigarettes ran out, and we fell back on rolling used tea-leaves in signal forms, the paper tasting worse than the tea-leaves. But however rank, such a fag was a change of smell.

By day I crawled from section to section when the company was forward, watching that the water ration was being sensibly eked out, passing on news of activities elsewhere in the battalion or brigade, lying beside the sentry/sniper to spot any movement on the slopes of Brig's Peak and Sanchil. It was important to talk with the men as much as possible and to listen to what they had to say, even if the conversation were limited to bad jokes. Then back to platoon HQ and the telephone, the line so often cut by shellfire and always quickly mended. By night there was more activity and freer movement; barbed wire had been lugged up, and had to be erected in the ravine, and subsequently the gaps mended; sections were changed round, the rations and ammunition taken over from the carrying company and distributed, casualties evacuated, the dead buried with loose stones and a few handfuls of earth. Every so often down would come a salvo, and as the days passed one jumped more at each burst. The tin hat became, almost obsessively, the only protection available: I remember lying at night, moving my tin hat from my head to my chest to my belly and back again as I reviewed my calculations as to where I would least like to be hit—a silly game one was ashamed to play in daylight.

At least the carrying was easier on our second sojourn on Cameron Ridge, for the Sappers had fixed up a do-it-yourself railway, with a 15-cwt. truck, whose wheels just straddled the permanent way, pulling a loaded flat up the incline to our section of the track. This cut out about half the haul from the floor of the valley, and meant that the wounded, once carried in agony down to the line, could have a relatively smooth run down to the station a few kilometres back. The flats coasted back on their own, relying on the rather dicky handbrake fitted to them. There was a bad accident one night when the brake failed and the flat ran away, and Sgt. Kane of D Company tried to stop it with his foot; he lost a leg and died soon after.

Much of our time was spent peering from the forward posts at Brig's Peak and Sanchil and looking for possible paths down into the ravine and up the other side, since we knew that the next step was to be an attack by both divisions, with the Camerons launching off from our own Ridge. Where was the enemy wire, the machine-gun positions? On those vast slopes, it was like looking for a stag in ten square miles of forest, with the difference that the beasts were looking down on us, and we up at them.

It was dismaying that no progress had been made, although no one thought that our commanders could or should have fought the battle otherwise; there was no way of by-passing the Keren massif, we had to batter our way through it. Then we heard that Wavell had flown down from Egypt to have a look at Keren and hear the plan for the next attack. The news flashed round the battalion and with it a surge of optimism; however difficult it might prove, this time we'd get through. There can never have been a general so averse as Wavell to the devisings of the P.R.O. mind, who was so completely not the popularity-hunter, yet never one who so commanded the confidence and affection of his soldiers.

Just as we were about to come off the hill while the Fusiliers took over, Alan George doubled up and collapsed with what turned out to be acute appendicitis, so bang went yet another of my company commanders. After we had been back in rest for a couple of days, Harry Cumming-

Bruce, a Seaforth, arrived and went to A Company, releasing David Douglas, to our huge satisfaction, to come back to command of C Company. Once again we cleaned up, looked to our kit and weapons, and did a little sweating up and down the nearest hill to limber up our legs. It wasn't all work—we had a very successful and splendidly uninhibited battalion concert party—but we knew that the Keren stalemate was somehow or another to be broken, and after the repulse of previous attacks were equally sure it was going to be a rough ride.

But there was no point in talking too much about it, something Andy grasped when he gave his orders to all the officers and NCOs of the battalion beside a sandtable model of the peaks we knew so well. Orders always start with information about the enemy and our own troops, to set the scene before giving the object—'Camerons will capture and hold Brig's Peak and Sanchil'—and method. Andy realized we knew quite enough of the strength, positions and determination of the Italian forces, and contented himself by saying with a grin at the outrageous lie he was uttering, 'Information about the enemy: the enemy is all wind and piss.'

On the night of March 19th we marched back and were up on Cameron Ridge by midnight in our assault positions, forward of the Raj Rif; C and B the leading companies, objectives Brig's Peak and Sanchil respectively. It was a long wait to 7 a.m. which was zero hour, but it gave us a chance to rest, since we were carrying extra bandoliers of ammunition and grenades. We had also been issued with artillery screens, big coloured panels to show our F.O.O.s the position of the leading troops. I was both cold and sweaty, the result of fear and exertion, and lost my signet ring as I went round the sections, which struck me as unlucky. The previous day I had tetchily refused to accept a letter to his parents from Jamesy Cameron of A Company, telling him to find a safer carrier, and I now had a very uncomfortable feeling that I had been right. He had been right too, poor fellow, for he was killed almost at once in the morning.

David's plan was for 13 and 14 Platoons to climb abreast, 15 Platoon between but behind them; he and company HQ would move up the hill to an agreed area when the advance had reached a certain point. We all were very clear that the only chance of pulling it off was to move as fast as possible down into the ravine and up the precipitous slopes of Brig's Peak, since we hoped that the very steepness of the hill would prevent the enemy artillery from landing anything on its forward slope. Apart from that, the safest place as far as enemy shelling is concerned is in amongst the enemy positions. There was no need to repeat any orders, all that remained was to make silly jokes in whispers as a rum ration was handed round. With only two officers in the company, we were short of platoon commanders, and Sgt. Ramage was moved to the command of 14 Platoon. I cannot remember who took over from him as my platoon sergeant in 15.

At 7 the barrage came down; to us, at that stage of the war, it seemed an unbelievable concentration of shellfire. We pelted forward, but as we ran we could see the whole line of crests before us blotted out in dust from the explosions. In moments the enemy guns replied, putting a counter barrage down on the ravine, the worst of which we escaped because of the speed with which we ran down into it and across it, but which hit B Company hard, on our right. Then we were climbing and the guns couldn't reach us, but the mortars could; the noise was shattering, but commands were unnecessary—every Jock knew that the only way was on up, leaving the wounded where they fell. Easier said than done; it was so steep, the mortar bombs on the lower slope were incessant, and were succeeded higher up the hill by cross-fire from machine guns enfilading the wire, and by showers of hand grenades thrown by Italians and Eritreans who had bravely sat tight in their forward posts. By the time we got through the barbed wire we had suffered a lot of casualties, and I had the remains of two platoons with me; Sgt. Ramage was the only NCO left. We had cleaned out half a dozen posts, disarming prisoners and chasing them off down the hill on their own, when our guns lifted the barrage; this enabled us to scramble the last thirty or forty yards to the top. The very summit was a pinnacle of bare rock, but we got round the side of it, which seemed too good to be true.

By then we were a very small party. Sgt. Ramage went next, his tin hat blown off with the top of his head still in it, the brains slipping down the side of his face; the most indecent of all the deaths I saw. We were now down to three Jocks and myself. I don't believe by this time we felt exhaustion or even fear, but were angrily looking for someone else to shoot or bayonet. With Pte. Webster immediately behind me, we carried on further round the back of the Peak, which seemed a good idea at the time: a brilliant flash, complete darkness and really agonizing pain in every part of my body at once. I came round, convinced I was blind until I scraped some of the blood and grit from my face, and found myself beside a big rock. Webster was bending over me, blood pouring from a wound above his eyes, when another grenade buckled his legs and he fell beside me.

It was uncannily quiet after the noise of the attack. We lay wondering if there were any more Camerons about. Voices—but Italian, and rifles poking us to get moving. Since neither of us could stand—both my legs and one arm were out of action— and after some arguing, we were carried to their regimental aid post, in a cave just below the summit. Here a young man picked out some of the bigger pieces of metal, bandaged us up, and had us laid under a rock in the shade; the heat was blistering. The two remaining soldiers in the party had been taken prisoner, I was told, but I couldn't see them.

Our captors were the Savoy Grenadiers, and when I saw

the number of troops about, I was sure that C Company, or what was left of it, would never be able to hold ground taken at the summit. Once again, it was the near impossibility on these enormous hills of getting enough men on to the objective to make an impact; if we had arrived at the top with fifty men instead of half a dozen, C Company might have done the trick.

As it was, with a shattering crash the barrage came down again, so it was obvious that the attack had failed and that we were not in position on the crests. But it wasn't possible to reflect on how the battle as a whole was going, for I was in too much pain and too frightened by the British gunfire, heavy and prolonged. The shells either hit the crest and its forward slope or screamed over our heads to pitch far down the mountain side towards the plain of Keren. The aid post, tucked in under the summit, was only hit by ricochets of rock and shell fragments until the R.A.F. took a hand and dive-bombed the positions behind the crest. We spent two days and a night lying beside our rock, the bombardment almost incessant to cover, as I learned later, the re-grouping of the shattered assault force and 5th Indian Division's attack on the right of the road block. By the second night, when the Italians decided to move us, I would have given anything to get off the hill.

Webster could hobble, his arm round a man's neck, but I kept passing out as two men tried to carry me down, so my escort impressed a passing mule and loaded me on to it. The track was as rough and steep as that on our side of the hill, and despite their care I fell off the mule three times. By now the hillside was less steep, and I was carried on a stretcher into a big tunnel on the railway line. Nothing could have been kinder than the Italians' behaviour to wounded prisoners. Up on top, their water ration was clearly as scanty as our own, but ungrudgingly they gave us swigs from their water bottles. My watch was left on my wrist, indeed it was helping to hold it together, and all I lost was the contents of my haversack when our equipment was unbuckled to save weight.

As well as a number of wounded men, the tunnel was crammed with stores and soldiers, the latter very interested in the prisoners and anxious to make conversation. I didn't wish to appear ungracious, but was incapable of making the effort required to talk beyond asking Webster whether he felt any better than I did. We were given coffee and offered bread, though neither of us could eat. Our guns must have been trying to register the railway, for a couple of shells burst right at the mouth, sending clouds of dust and cordite fumes into the tunnel and creating pandemonium. One man jumped for cover on top of my legs in the confusion, and I knew no more for some time.

After twenty-four hours there, a stretcher party carried us and other wounded by night down from the railway into the gorge and up to the main road behind the vast road block. Luckily our guns weren't shelling the road at the time, and ambulances ran us back to a field hospital, and then back to the main hospital at Asmara.

Unlike previous affrays, we had gone into this battle with no divisional or regimental identifications; the Camerons had even been ordered to leave off our little scarlet garter flashes, as signifying a Highland regiment. At the field hospital I was questioned closely by an intelligence officer while my wounds were being dressed, which illogically seemed unfair, particularly in conjunction with a good deal of joking by the medical orderlies that a few centimetres' variation in the flight of some of the grenade fragments would have turned me into a *castrato*. I stuck to instructions—the only information permissible is name, rank, number; and evidently Webster did likewise, since the I.O. came back twice. A third time he appeared to tell me in triumph that I belonged to the Queen's Own Cameron Highlanders, that our badge was St. Andrew with his cross, and that *Nemo me impune lacessit* was of some significance to us; it transpired that Webster's torn shirt had revealed a masterpiece in three colours of the tattoo-ist's art.

It took some time in the Asmara hospital to take in where I was; when I eventually got my bearings, I found myself in a bed for the first time in months, in a small ward with barred windows. There were two other prisoners, at the convalescent stage, George Reaney of the 25th Field Regiment R.A., who had been wounded and captured early in the advance, and John Littlehailes of the King's African Rifles, hit in the campaign on Ethiopia's southern frontier. They were avid for news. I was a gloomy but inaccurate prophet: Keren was an immensely strong defensive position, with no way round it, and thus only open to head-on battering. Although enemy casualties were heavy, as the hospital bore witness, we seemed to be having more of a battering than the Italians, and I thought it would be months before we broke through. It turned out to be three weeks.

The hospital was very short of supplies — anaesthetics were reserved for amputations — but I had exactly the same treatment as the Italian wounded. This consisted for me of a daily dressing of wounds, with much probing for grenade fragments. The surgeon wanted to make a big incision above one knee; I was given a shot of brandy and a plug of bandage to chew on, a burly orderly sat on my chest and another on my feet, and the surgeon carried on. After a fortnight a disagreeable smell was apparent in our ward, reminiscent of the decomposing bodies at Keren; my legs had turned gangrenous. I soon ceased to notice the smell, but it must have been disgusting for the others. The surgeon offered me a choice between amputating both legs and survival, or cutting off the rotten bits of flesh with odds against its working. I opted for the latter, but the method was so intensely painful that I would start weeping an hour or so before his daily treatment.

Food was also short, or so the others told me; it was a matter of indifference to me, as was their weekly cigarette ration—a large leaf of Ethiopian tobacco which they carefully separated from the ribs and stalk and then rolled up. It was so strong that they lay down on their beds before lighting up. Hospital routine was of course erratic in the circumstances, and we were left alone most of the time, an orderly occasionally bringing in a newspaper, which promised that yet another English city would be *conventrizzata*—the Italians were officially immensely proud of having been allowed to take part in the Coventry raid. Refreshingly, the orderly looked on the official view as a sick joke, though he looked on his duties in much the same light. One night after we had been locked up, the partly-healed artery in my wrist opened up, pumping blood all over the bedding; George and John hammered on the door to get the orderly, who took in the situation at a glance and rushed off to fetch a pile of rags, to protect the blankets.

The surgeons and nurses were worked off their feet and had no time for talk but we were visited one day by a Franciscan, whose French or English was as sketchy as our Italian. He resolved the problem by resolutely addressing me 'O miles' and sticking to Latin.

One day we heard gunfire, we could see through our barred window columns of smoke from the outskirts of Asmara as dumps were destroyed; everybody on the hospital staff suddenly sported Red Cross armbands, and the 5th Indian rolled through the city without opposition. An Indian Army medical unit took over the hospital. The Colonel commanding it examined me. His wise brown face was topped with silvery hair; his charm and good manners couldn't prevent his nose wrinkling as he bent over my legs, so I knew I must still smell pretty bad. He talked to one of the surgeons in his unit, Charles Bliss, a wild Irishman whom I later got to know well, and in no time I was being operated on, this time with anaesthetic. Thanks to them, I survived the gangrene with two perfectly usable legs, and hardly a day has passed since then without my feeling actively grateful to them.

The Indian unit moved on with the army, being replaced by a General Hospital. A sister like an RSM took over our wing, which was filthy; she ran the Italian orderlies ragged, until they must have longed for the comparative *dolce vita* of Fascismo. She got down to essentials at once: 'When did you last have a bowel movement, Mr. Cochrane?'

'Four weeks ago, Sister,' I could truthfully reply, the only occasion on which I have succeeded in flattening the nursing profession.

By this time there had been flocks of visitors, I think every officer in the battalion from Andy downwards, and I was brought up to date on the news. The most welcome visitors of all were David Douglas and Wattie Reid, for I had spent the weeks wondering how they or anybody in C Company had survived. Very few did, unwounded. The battalion lost eight officers and 250 other ranks in the battle of Keren. C Company had suffered 50 casualties in the final attack on Brig's Peak. David, with ten men, had held for twenty-four hours the ground we had over-run on the slope below Brig's Peak until forced to pull back for lack of water and reinforcements—every man on two feet was already fully committed. It was much the same with B Company on the right, attacking Sanchil, and D Company to the left going for a ridge called Hog's Back. On the Camerons' left the Raj Rif had got a footing on Hog's Back, further left the Mahrattas got to Flat Top, but in neither case had they sufficient survivors to exploit their success. From Sanchil and Brig's Peak murderous fire was directed onto the 5th Indian Division's attack to the right of the gorge and road block; the fighting continued for another ten bitter days until our old tunnel was cleared of its blockage of wrecked wagons, and the Highland Light Infantry made a surprise attack through it, simultaneouly with a move along the right hand side of the gorge by the West Yorks. This gave the Sappers and Miners a chance to clear the landslide and make a twelve-foot roadway across it, thirty-six hours non-stop work, mostly under fire. With that the battle was almost over, and the Italians began to withdraw in good order; but they had been so hammered that there was little resistance until the final stand under the Duke of Aosta at Ambi-Alagi in northern Ethiopia.

After the battle, the bodies of nineteen Cameron Highlanders were found, and buried, on the summits of Sanchil and Brig's Peak, in addition to all those killed on the slopes leading up to them and in the weeks of fighting before the final assault; David told me who had been killed or wounded, and how seriously. Fortunately a large draft of six officers and 158 other ranks had arrived, so the battalion was again operational—as well, since the whole 4th Indian Division was wanted urgently back in the Western Desert; the Germans were pouring troops into North Africa, and Wavell had been saddled with the débâcle in Greece.

Meanwhile the battalion was employed on that most loathsome of tasks, cleaning up the battlefield; salvage was the euphemistic term for what mostly consisted of burying people who had been dead for a long time. Andy of course stumped round the hills, encouraging the Jocks —this I heard from Wattie who always had a story to cheer one up: 'Well, how's it going, Macpherson?'

'I'm daein' fine, sir, except I've got twa buckshee heids.'

Webster recovered fairly quickly, and I didn't see him again, so the moment when David and Wattie left the ward was my last direct contact with the old C Company. Within days they were on the way back to the Sudan, to Suez, back to the desert. Within two months of leaving Keren they were up to the neck in the bitter fighting at Halfaya Pass, where David was one of the many casualties, though fortunately only wounded. The battalion was heavily involved during the winter of 1941–2 in the swirling desert campaign, culminating in three brilliantly executed rearguard actions. The finale was in June 1942, when the brigade was sent with the South African Division into Tobruk, a fortress that had been denuded of its minefield defences.

By now Andy was commanding the brigade and Colin Duncan the battalion, which fought with great distinction while the German attack over-ran the rest of the defences. The anti-tank guns had a field day, a corporal and his gun crew knocking out six tanks in a row during one attack, and spirits were so high that the battalion refused to accept as serious a message that the garrison had surrendered. A German emissary with two South African officers confirmed that this was the case, and that only the Camerons were still fighting; and gave the C.O. until 5 next morning to surrender. Colin Duncan's response was that he doubted whether many of his officers and men would care to parade at so early an hour. During the night, after everything usable had been destroyed, fifteen officers and 200 men set out in small parties to walk back to wherever the British line had been stablized. Most were picked up in days, since the area was swarming with Germans, but some covered the 500 miles to Alamein, with astounding adventures on their trek.

Colin Duncan stayed with the unfit or wounded who couldn't attempt the break-out, and at 5 a.m. on June 22nd duly paraded the remnant of his battalion. Not for them the hang-dog shuffle into captivity of the defeated; under Colin the Camerons marched in, headed by their pipers.

5

INTERLUDE

I SPENT a couple of months in the hospital after the battalion had gone, and then another two months in a rest camp in Asmara waiting for a ship, since I had been 'sat on' by a Medical Board and recommended six months' leave in South Africa on the ground that Egypt was too hot for convalescence. There was no mail from home because letters still went to the battalion, and it was a weary, tedious wait, alleviated by the daily pleasure of finding that I could flex my wrist and fingers and use my legs more and more until I finally dispensed with every aid but a walking stick. Asmara held little of interest—a cathedral, handsome government buildings, one or two broad streets with shops, hotels and bars all equally empty; some fine villas and a shanty town on the outskirts.

It was unkindly said that the incoming British administration took three immediate steps: started laying out a golf course, re-opened the city brothel under careful medical supervision, and ordered all traffic to drive on the left. The last measure must have caused almost as many casualties as the campaign, since there were still plenty of enormous Italian lorries on the road, and the drivers found some difficulty in remembering the rule.

Occasional trips into the countryside almost justified being stuck in Asmara, for the roads and the views were both spectacular. In particular I remember a journey into northern Ethiopia, where I drove in a commandeered Alfa Romeo with a friend whose job was to salvage Italian transport. At Amba-Alagi, scene of the last stand and final surrender, there was a vast pile of weapons, ammunition and vehicles guarded by a

79

detachment of King's African Rifles, who fought nightly battles with the locals. We found ourselves involved in ferocious exchanges of fire with the would-be looters, anxious to equip themselves for a descent on their un-armed neighbours. Amba-Alagi itself was a towering height, fortified with ingenuity and able to stand a long siege had the water supply matched the stocks of food and ammunition.

It was the finest countryside I have ever seen, the more striking in contrast to Eritrea's savage sterility. The scale was enormous, the air so clear that it was difficult to realize the distance from one mountain range to the next, green to the summits. In the valleys rolling meadows, miles across, lay between wooded hillocks, dotted with villages of little beehive houses. The light had a curious blue-green tone, precisely like a Claude painting. To heighten the effect were the necessary groups of figures in the foreground, Jephthah's or Moses's to a man; un-like a Claude, the figures were as likely to be dangerous as picturesque.

I got to know an Italian family in Decamere, near Asmara, and spent a good deal of time with them; Signor Danieli had once been an Alfa racing driver, and had come to Eritrea to manage a transport service and repair depot. He was interesting on the differences between the Eritreans and the Ethiopians, and the Italian attitude towards them. Although Eritrea had been a colony so long, no Italian bothered to learn the language, even in the army, which was why in every tiny village we found Eritreans with a fair command of Italian. The poor whites lived on the edge of the city in shanties no whit better than those of the subject people, a sort of egalitarianism in misery which perhaps was a compensation for colonialism, and was strikingly unusual to British eyes. Apart from *shifta* or bandits in the hills, preying upon the people and the colonists indiscrimi-nately, there appeared to have been a tolerably relaxed atmosphere, whereas in Ethiopia the Italians were evidently very frightened. My acquaintance told me that in fifty years the settlers there would not have been able to live or work without military protection.

I remember being introduced at their dining table to the taste of prickly pears, stripped from the giant cactus, divested of their spikes and eaten with a drop of brandy; but I cannot remember anything of the Danieli family conversation which my diary tantalizingly records as 'too broad for any mess or club'.

I had one formal parade in Asmara, when Wavell flew in. Lt. P. S. Bhagat of the 21st Royal Bombay Sappers, who had performed an astonishingly brave feat in clearing mines by hand while under fire, had been awarded the V.C., and I the D.S.O.; and we were both ordered to parade to have medal ribbons pinned on. I was suffering from an acute attack of gippy tummy, the only cure for which is to drink brandy after it has been burned for some moments (in another glass or cup, if you don't want to scorch your lips). My innards sealed like concrete by this infallible remedy, I duly paraded at 10 a.m., reeking of brandy. Wavell must have thought me an exceptionally dissolute second lieutenant, but contented himself with a heart-warming encomium on the Camerons.

Eventually in the middle of August 1941 I got away, travelling down to Massawa to sail for Suez in a dirty little steamer, all tattered red plush and no ventilation. It was crowded with South African soldiers, burly men oppressed by the heat; in Massawa it was well over 120° in the shade, and the Red Sea afforded no relief. The deck was packed with men kicking and floundering with heat stroke, and three of them died. At Suez I had news of the battalion, and heard of its casualties at Halfaya Pass, and the fact that David had won the D.S.O. I spent a night at the transit camp revolving the idea of smuggling myself up to the battalion, but found in the morning that I couldn't put myself to the fence; as well, for I would have been little use and it would have been a silly piece of false heroics. So the *Mauretania* took me and a thousand or two others down the Red Sea again in comfort, and I disembarked at Durban on September 3rd. It seemed very cold.

The hospital, little brick huts with an iron roof, was just outside Pietermaritzburg, the capital of Natal. We were treated with the greatest kindness, given the run of the club, invited out to people's homes, and regaled with stories of the iniquities of Durban, the flaming infamy of Johannesburg. The people of this pleasant, sleepy little town were filled with the envious venom that comes from the feeling of having been left behind. I was fortunate in being asked to stay by the headmaster of Hilton College and his wife; the school stands in 16,000 of its own acres, over which we rode on little unshod Basuto ponies. This, and swimming, were a delight, but tennis was still for me a stationary game. The greatest pleasure of all was to be in a house full of books where the evenings were spent in music or in conversation, not talking shop.

There had been little talk of politics in Pietermaritzburg. At that time the extreme Afrikaaners were looked on, in Natal at any rate, as pro-German, *tout court*, without much analysis that I can recollect of their basic fascism which would outlive any pro-German or anti-British sentiment. Several of the convalescents in the hospital were so captivated by the beauty of South Africa and the generous kindness of our hosts that they vowed to come back and settle, but the signs on the park benches were such an affront, particularly to anyone who had served in an Indian division, and so true a reflection of the state of things, that I prophesied that the lid was bound to blow off in ten years. I was quite wrong, not realizing, to continue the metaphor, what immense forces could be held down by pressure cooking.

I was re-called from Hilton College to the hospital, to find my first mail from home for five months, and to be told that instead of local leave I was to sail for Britain in twenty-four hours' time. Rush and rapture, a hurried journey back to Durban and the *Christiaan Huygens*, a Dutch liner on which my father had often travelled to and from Java. The captain indeed asked me after a day or two's observation whether my name were not Cochrane, claiming that the likeness was unmistakeable.

It was a slow voyage, since we finally left Cape Town on October 5th, and reached Nova Scotia on the 28th, to spend ten days in dry dock at St. John, where again the kindness was overwhelming, though the weather dismal. Back to Halifax, where we loaded up with R.A.F. boys who had been taught to fly in Canada and the U.S.A., and in convoy with a large naval escort we crossed the Atlantic. By the time I was demobilized, I had spent five and a half months at sea in troopships of one sort and another, more than four of those months during hostilities. There was never a sign of enemy action, though one or two alarms, which brought home the reality of command of the sea, and the magnitude of the Navy's success in retaining it. The worst feature of any troopship voyage was the horrifying disparity between the accommodation for officers and for men; in a hospital ship, one's conscience could at least be easy on that score. I was sharing a cabin with an officer in the King's Dragoon Guards, a passionate Wagner lover, who had nipped down to New York while we were docked in St. John to get some new Flagstadt records. He lashed his gramophone to the lavatory seat in the bathroom next door, and we pitched and rolled across the Altantic accompanied by the diva's imperious and superb singing.

We docked at Liverpool on November 22nd, conveniently since my family was then living there, and the convalescents were taken to Ormskirk Hospital where a Medical Board swiftly pronounced on us. 'Category C, four weeks leave' was my verdict, and I shuffled away in exhilaration to join my parents and my sister, Marigold.

* * *

The Camerons' depot in Inverness had been taken over by the Auxiliary Territorial Service and I found myself in shared quarters at Fort George, the Seaforths' depot; a foretaste of the highly successful amalgamation of the two regiments after the war to form The Queen's Own Highlanders. Fort George is an exception to the common rule of preposterously turretted Victorian barracks, since it was largely built by John and Robert Adams on Vaubanesque lines. Within the massive walls of the fort, on a ground plan like the Star of David, stand blocks of agreeable eighteenth-century buildings; it is true that at that time the barrack accommodation and sanitation were still much of the period. The Fort stands on a spit sticking into the Moray Firth, with fine views across the water to the Black Isle. My duties were nominal, since I wasn't fit enough to train the conscripts, and I was told to do whatever I thought would make me well.

This meant, as soon as spring arrived, fishing. Proprietors were generous in granting permission to fish their lochs and rivers, the only problem being transport. I seriously thought of going half-shares with another keen angler in a pony and trap, but then we met a third fisherman in the R.A.F. who could land his aeroplane in, it seemed, the smallest of fields. Fishing led to golf and in turn to the ability to dance an eightsome without falling down, which inevitably led to a posting. If you can dance a reel, as danced on a mess night, you are fit enough to fight anyone.

The posting was not a regimental one, unfortunately, but to an Officer Cadet Training Unit in Wales. The cadets were not superb material, but better training by a better staff of officers would have made something of

ASMARA: Gen. Sir Archibald Wavell and
2nd. Lieut. Cochrane

ERITREA: After the Action at Agordat

St. Mark's, North Audley Street, 14 September 1943

them; as it was, it was a miserable unit. The news that the 2nd Camerons had disappeared in the fall of Tobruk made it intolerable and I volunteered for the Parachute Regiment to get out of the place. Whether I would have been accepted, or whether my legs would have stood up to jumping, were never put to the test, for I was summoned to the War Office and told that in forty-eight hours I was to leave for Washington as a delegate to an International Students Assembly—'You were at Oxford when the war started, weren't you? Good, you'll do.'

This was the introduction to an astonishing couple of months which have never lost their dream-like fantasy in contrast with the years of war before and after. Three of us went: Richard Miles, a naval officer, and David Scott-Malden of the R.A.F., who had both like me been up at university in 1939. Between us we mustered quite a range of active service, the real reason for our abrupt dispatch, for the Russians had decided to send a much-decorated delegation to the Assembly. Until then it had been ignored by the British Embassy in Washington.

We left Bristol on August 28th in the aftermath of an air raid, and flew to Shannon, wearing civvies of course, strange garb after two years of khaki; a bus to Foynes and a launch trip to a Sikorski four-engined Pan-Am flying boat. It was the only really comfortable Atlantic crossing I have ever made. There was space enough on two decks to walk about, and at bedtime one retired to an elegant bunk, getting between sheets in one's pyjamas. On landing we taxied up to one of the Manhattan piers and came ashore like mariners, none of the noise and confusion and swarming crowds of Heathrow or Kennedy. The confusion was in fact all our own, lessened when a kind man from the Information Office in New York, Ed Brown, met us, fended off reporters, took us to his apartment where we went mad at the sight of a bowl of bananas, and gave up his Sunday afternoon to driving us round until it was time to catch a train for Washington.

Ed was the first example of a recurring phenomenon, the very efficient and wholly delightful American citizen who had been recruited by the British for the various missions, consulates and information offices; this showed surprising acumen, for on the whole the only disagreeable people we met in our two months stay were the British officials in those missions, etc. Not wholly accurate; in many cases their wives were even more disagreeable. It was ironical to find in Washington that the most offensively 'English' of the Embassy wives was in fact Irish.

The train was packed, and we had heard that the capital was so overcrowded that it would be impossible to find an hotel room. An affable Marine sergeant heard our discussion on the merits of park benches versus the station waiting-room, and promised to slip us into his barracks. But at Union Station we walked into the arms of a welcoming deputation, which included Louise Morley, my future wife, and were directed to an enormous motor car which was to whisk us to the White House. We had some trouble finding our kind sergeant to explain that we were OK, indeed rather more than OK, for accommodation; 'Don't let the President give you any wooden nickels' was his farewell remark.

Mrs. Roosevelt was actively interested in the Assembly, and this was the first of her many acts of kindness to us. To find ourselves in luxurious guest rooms in the White House, three days after being pulled in from our respective Nissen huts, was so wildly improbable that we lay on our beds in helpless laughter. To have a swim before breakfast next morning in a borrowed pair of the President's bathing pants heightened the air of unreality, which wasn't dispelled by being taken on tours of Washington by the First Lady. On one of them she sent us on ahead to the Capitol with the chauffeur because she had to go somewhere to inspect a bust—'I am *always* going to look at busts of my husband' she exclaimed—and caught us up in the Rotunda. She immediately gathered us under her wing to explain things; it was the nicest thing in the world to see her reactions as she was recognized. She bowed and bobbed to the people, 'Good morning', 'Good morning', with her very lovely smile, and a big wave as we left; no false modesty, she was the wife of the President of the United States and knew she was instantly recognizable, yet unmistakeably gave the impression that she felt none of this accrued to her as a person, or was very important. We were her total devotees in hours. She became someone like a very favourite aunt, warm-hearted, amusing, and formidably shrewd behind the platitudes she appeared to use as a smoke screen when she was with more than half a dozen people.

The International Students Assembly was planned as a gesture of 'youth in the free world' against the Axis, and it was attacked so violently by the Nazis that we began to take it seriously. We had to parade at the Embassy beforehand. Halifax, then the Ambassador, was worth going a long way to meet; enormously tall, a movingly ascetic face, burningly sincere and deeply anxious to see other people's point of view. But we grew rather incensed at being told elsewhere in the Embassy what we should and should not say, which is probably why our first full-blown press conference found us skating over some very thin ice regarding our views on Britain after the war.

The Assembly itself consisted of lectures and group discussions on every aspect of the post-war world, into which we entered with a gusto I'd forgotten since Oxford. Apart from broad declarations like the Atlantic Charter, 'war aims' were something we all held as individuals. I can remember nobody who thought the world of the thirties worth resurrecting; but how would we change it? The best of the talk was far into the night at the American University, where we now were billeted in more realistic quarters than in the White House. What we said in

speeches or at press conferences was certainly not particularly official and couldn't claim to represent the views of
the British student body, if such an amorphous thing did
or does exist, but that didn't inhibit us in the least. The
climax was a ringing declaration signed by us all, except
the Norwegians who overslept that day; the wording of
the declaration caused much manoeuvring and politick-
ing since it included a reference to the rights of all people
to independence. This was a fine swipe at colonialism
insisted on by the Russians, who thereupon refused to
sign if a Lithuanian student were allowed to sign too. It
was a very educative Assembly.

The President addressed it, but in a broadcast since the
Secret Service were against his going in person to any
gathering of more than fifty people. Some of us were
invited to the White House to meet him, and to listen
to him making his broadcast. He radiated a sense of
energy and power, even in the few words he spoke to us
individually. He addressed us collectively, just before the
red light went on at his desk, in thoroughly practical
terms: 'Don't sneeze.'

We got to know the Russians very well in the next
couple of months. There were three of them: Ludmilla
Pavlichenko who had performed prodigies as a sniper
behind the German lines; Vladimir Pchelintsev, also a
sniper, who had been an engineering student in 1941;
and the leader, Nikolai Krasavchenko, who despite his
youth had been in charge of fuel distribution in Moscow
the previous winter. Always in close attendance was a
horrible little man from the Soviet Embassy, the official
interpreter. Ludmilla, who spoke only Russian, was a
placid, stout girl who looked well in her smart uniform;
the interpreter wouldn't let her discuss how she shot her
Germans, 309 no less, which I think was all she really
wanted to talk about. Vladimir spoke some German,
and was always giving the bear-leader trouble, for he
enjoyed a party and was an enthusiastic and accom-

plished dancer. Like us, he clearly thought this was a miraculous break in a war we were all returning to, and he wasn't going to waste a moment of it. He had a perfect command of two English phrases, 'No thank you, I don't smoke', and 'I love you', and with them he swept the board. Nikolai was the dark horse. He understood English but wouldn't admit to it, or speak it. Like a good emissary, all he said or did was planned in advance; once one knew the party line, one could answer all the questions put to him before he and the interpreter could do so, which irritated them both profoundly, the more so in that the answers were always 'correct'. The only thing that cracked his façade was his sense of humour which occasionally got the better of the carefully-drilled public self. Not all jokes are verbal, and when one got under his guard he would laugh until he wept. Then he dried his eyes, apologized, and once more assumed the functionary.

After the Assembly some of the overseas delegates were formed into two teams and sent off to visit universities and colleges up and down the States. Before we split up Richard and David and I had some time in New York, and the first of several enchanted weekends with Mrs. Roosevelt at Val-Kil, her little house on the Roosevelt estate at Hyde Park. Getting there involved a train ride, with superb views across the Hudson, to Poughkeepsie where we were met by Mr. Schaeffer, the driver and handyman whom we got to know fairly well. He was very informative, with a fruity Bronx accent. 'Dem boids,' he told us on our first trip, 'dem boids is poitridges.' Sometimes Mrs. Roosevelt and her secretary Miss Thomson were there on their own, which was particularly enjoyable; sometimes there was other company—Trude Pratt, who had been much involved in the Assembly, and Joe Lash who has since written such a superb biography of Mrs. Roosevelt, or Army officers from the Hyde Park guard. Either way, the weekends were a delight in that pretty house with its good garden, a lake, a swimming pool, books, and endless good talk. Mrs. R. sometimes took us out—to Hyde Park itself, to see the President's books and keepsakes, and to dinner with the Morgenthaus, down the Hudson. Henry Morgenthau was then Secretary of the Treasury, and was having a rough time with Congress over some very stringent measures he had proposed. The family were all sitting head in hand when we arrived which Mrs. Morgenthau explained by saying, 'We were just trying to figure how we can possibly live if Henry's tax laws go through,'

It was hard to say whether our time at Val-Kil or in New York was more bewilderingly out of the wartime world we knew. The city positively glittered in our eyes, brilliantly lit at night, gleaming in the daytime sunshine, the shop windows packed with everything that at home was unattainable. We did the sights, from Coney Island to the Empire State Building and the Met. We watched the Dodgers play the Pirates, kind neighbours in the stand explaining the finer points of the game, but differently, so that rival factions came to fisticuffs as we cowered in our seats. David and I did the town with two girls from the Assembly, Louise Morley and Jane Plimpton, from dinner at the St. Regis Roof to the theatre, to a boogie-woogie joint in Greenwich Village, on to Cafe Society Uptown and, when everything else put the shutters up, to a Hamburger Heaven where the cook turned out to be a Moroccan who had fought under Abd el Krim against the French. Fortunately there was a place in New York where I could get advances on my pay, which meant penury for months and months to come.

New York bars were an enormous improvement on the dingy pubs at home; apart from being clean and cheerful, they actually had drink to sell. On a hot day we asked in one for a refreshing drink to which we had been introduced, a Cuba Libre, rum with coke and a slice of lime. 'What rum?' asked the bar-tender. The junior services deferred to the Navy's expertise: 'What rums have you got?' asked Richard. Nettled, the man put out bottle after bottle, ranging from dark mahogany to colourless spirit. 'No good just looking at them, pour me a jigger of each,' and Richard solemnly drank his way through nine tots. 'The fourth bottle, please', and our Cuba Libres were duly made. Richard maintained a ramrod carriage until we got him back to our hotel; the bar-tender was so tickled that he gave us a drink on the house whenever we returned to his establishment.

But high jinks came to an end with the departure of the two tours. David and Richard, with Ludmilla and a Dutch naval officer, were despatched to the West Coast, while Nikolai and Vladimir, Miss Wang, who was a Chinese actress of exceptional beauty, a Javanese dancer named Abdul Kader and I set off on a very exhausting trip through New England, then as far into the Middle West as Michigan and south to Tennessee. Our charming and efficient 'manager' was a girl from Holyoke, Irene Murray, who couldn't get used to being addressed trisyllabically. Alas, Louise, of whom I had been seeing as much as possible since the Assembly, was managing the western tour. Ours was a very curious team, and I can't think that what we had to say did much to enlighten our audiences about the war's effects on other countries, although nobody threw anything at us, and indeed we sometimes evoked positive enthusiasm.

The drill was usually to stay in a college overnight, split up amongst the faculty or in fraternity houses, gassing away till the small hours. Next day there followed a speech-making session and questions and answers, and then a dash to catch a train. We varied the routine by spending night after night in sleeping cars. Irene had the fearsome task of scheduling, but even she found it difficult to keep to the timetable when broadcasts and press conferences were interpolated by over-zealous hosts. The pattern was different in places like Boston or Detroit where there would be a couple of large public meetings as well, much more alarming than college assemblies.

The United States had been directly in the war for only eight months and in some respects was only just, it seemed, coming round after the profound national shock of Pearl Harbor and the loss of the Philippines. We learned that in some quarters the war did not have that sense of the inevitable which it had for us and our contemporaries, with the vileness of Nazi-ism on our doorstep. One of the reasons that the International Student Service organized these tours round the colleges, I was told later, was to make the point that war was bound to affect students personally, that nowadays you couldn't hire other people to fight a war for you. If this did need to be underlined in colleges in 1942, our curious group may have helped to do so.

The questioning was usually sympathetic, although there were a good few misconceptions about Britain. Most people were amazed at how total was our war effort. I was fortunate here in being able to fall back on my own family as an example. My father, an engineer, was responsible then for keeping the Liverpool docks functioning despite the bombing; my mother caught a train at 5.30 every morning to fill shells in an ordnance factory, while my sister was busy de-ciphering at Bletchley. India was a recurring subject, and here again I was lucky, for an explanation of the workings of an Indian division, part of the largest volunteer army known to history, appeared an effective rebuttal of some of the more lunatic theories of a sub-continent groaning in bondage. The Second Front, or lack of it, came up at almost every meeting, and particularly in the speeches made by Nikolai and Vladimir. Eventually I lost my temper and told the interpreter that the next time he implied on their behalf that Britain was delaying a Second Front in order to bleed the Soviet Union to death, I would deliver a harangue on the Nazi-Soviet Pact with an addendum on the Soviet invasion of Finland.

Miss Wang stirred the audiences by letting them look at her, while Abdul, wise fellow, used to dance instead of making speeches, so the oratory had to come from the Russians and me. What we said became very standardised since we had to perform so often; indeed I learned most of Vladimir's speech by heart after hearing it time after time, and one night convulsed him and Nikolai by spouting it at them with all the correct gestures. Our odd troupe got along very well despite the strain and rush of so hectic a tour. It contained many pleasures, notably that of watching the scenery from the train, for in those days America had a wonderful railroad system, fast, clean and comfortable, delicious food in the diners, good bunks in the sleeping cars. Its only defect for a stranger was that in the palatial city stations one had to ask for directions to find a place to buy a ticket and to board the train.

In the blur of places and people a few incidents stood out. One was having lunch with Henry Ford at the then new Willow Run plant, turning out a bomber a day on the assembly line. The old man was lively and very talkative. 'Do you see that building?' he asked, pointing to some far distant chimneys. 'That factory belongs to the Duponts. They're a greedy family, they're making money out of this war.' I objected that he had just told me how the U.S. Government had helped Ford's to build Willow Run and to create their own fleet of ore-carrying ships; surely it would be difficult for him to avoid making money out of the war? 'Young man, I may have some more plants as a result but I won't have a cent more in my bank account, so I *won't* be making money.'

From economics we passed to letters. Did I admire Tennyson? Had I read *Locksley Hall*? 'That is a poem which will live for a thousand years.' I rather jibbed at this. 'Young man, I know it will live for a thousand years because I'm having a million copies printed to make sure it does.'

93

After visiting twenty-three universities and colleges, it was good to get back to New York on October 23rd and unwind, to hear David and Richard's hilarious account of the western tour, and to see more of their late manager; this included the pleasure of staying on Long Island with her parents, Helen and Christopher Morley, who seemed unperturbed by what was very evidently in the wind. Whatever has happened since, thirty-five years ago New York must have been the most beautiful city in the world, as well as the friendliest. To be there in the crisply sunny fall, and in love, was a heady conjunction.

Back to the job; Richard was ordered to Washington as assistant naval attaché, David was flown home in a bomber from Canada and I crossed the Atlantic in a very small Norwegian ship with a heartening cargo of bacon and eggs. The Russian party had left just before for London, where an imitation of the Student Assembly was being put together. Louise was despatched as the American delegate. It was a good choice for many reasons, among them the fact that on the western tour she had become a close friend of Ludmilla, who in London was very properly feted. She clung to Louise for help and support, and her very touching and public demonstration of affection was an effective counter to those who seemed to think you could only be a Friend of the Soviet Union by being anti-American.

I had a couple of quick meetings with Louise in London before picking up the job of soldiering once more, but wasn't involved in any of the conference proceedings, at which I was delighted to read that Ludmilla had been presented with a pearl-handled pistol and a complete Shakespeare. In consequence I did not see Nikolai or Vladimir again. I wrote to them, in carefully innocuous terms, but never had a reply. There was better fortune with Richard and David, and we resumed our friendship in the shabby grime of post-war London, a world away from the fantasy and dottiness of our American trip.

6

NEW COMPANY

ON December 20th 1942 the 2nd Battalion was re-formed. This took the shape of re-numbering the existing 4th Battalion, one of the regiment's territorial army units which had been serving in the West Indies, and at that time was stationed in the Shetlands. Anyone who had been in the old 2nd was wanted, and I jumped at the opportunity of getting back to regimental soldiering. First and foremost among old friends I found there was David Douglas, who had been invalided home after recovering from his wounds at the Halfaya battle and had thus missed the catastrophe at Tobruk; and it was very good to see Toby Irvine again. I was put in charge of the Carrier Platoon, which entailed a pretence to greater mechanical knowledge than I possessed, and required an ability to drive the things, and to get about on a motor-bike which I found even more frightening to ride than a horse. The platoon's activities were pretty much limited to the island's road system, for any cross-country manoeuvring ended in disaster; indeed, one of the carriers on my strength was just a map reference in one of Shetland's limitless bogs. So I was delighted in a month or two to be put in command of C Company. The wheel was beginning to come round.

It was at that time a curious battalion. There were good officers and NCOs and men in it, but some of them were infected by an embarrassed sense of having spent, so far, a cushy war guard-mounting in Bermuda and Aruba. The battalion had no very clear role since it was highly unlikely that the Germans would land in the Shetlands, although there were occasional alarms of U boats putting in to the isolated voes or sea lochs, when we turned out and scurried over the hills. Its main task was to train for war, but because we were the only infantry force in the island, formation training with other units or with gunners and sappers wasn't feasible, though admittedly a Shetland 'battle school' had been set up. Worst of all, we had a commanding officer unsuited for the job on hand.

His appointment must have looked on the face of it an eminently sensible one. He was intelligent, a linguist, a man of great courage who had been parachuted into guerilla-held territory in Europe; he was a fanatic about the good name of the regiment, and determined to make his battalion a good one. Alas, he had no idea of how to get the best out of people, or even the second best, and could not communicate with his officers or men. When he was enthusiastic, he couldn't light the fire, and when he was displeased he escaped into a fit of the dismals instead of roaring out his anger and then forgetting the matter; and he was a fusser, always concentrating on the trivial and missing the major weaknesses he should have jumped on. He must have been eaten up with self-doubt, for he never gave any impression, on or off duty, of actually enjoying the command of the 2nd Battalion The Queen's Own Cameron Highlanders, and thus his command wasn't very enjoyable to anyone else.

Shetland in winter is cold and wet and very windy, with heavy gales blowing for a week at a time, carrying so much salt spray that one could see why the people built little stone-walled enclosures in which to grow their cabbage and kale. The billets, on the edge of Lerwick, were dilapidated huts, and it was difficult to get the company into shape; but who has ever thought he stepped into a well-run inheritance? I was certainly sure that there was much to be put right, with myself as company commander into the bargain, but I was not amused when the C.O. sent me to the battle school to learn what live ammunition sounded like. I was tempted to put some

rounds near the feet of the directing staff, but instead
shot a sheep, for we were hungry. There was a remarkable
fuss at which I pointed out that the execrable food at
their school must be intended to teach soldiers how to live
off the country, and that if their cooks were incapable of
skinning and butchering a ewe, they would have no place
on a battlefield.

From every point of view it was a relief to get away
from the C.O. and Lerwick when C Company was
ordered off on detachment to a little place called Voe—
some scattered crofts, a small tweed and knitting mill,
and, isolated by a mile or two, our group of Nissen huts.
Now we really could get down to work and make something of our excellent material. In almost every way
it was a different enterprise to the old C Company,
and not just because it held only a handful of regular
soldiers.

For a start there was the number of officers. In the old
days three officers in a company had been richness, but
now I had four, with two others attached. The second-
in-command was Ian Jack, a captain as was I by then.
He had started in the hotel business in the bad days of
the thirties, working for six months on a pound a week at
the Royal British in Edinburgh, and then another six
months on thirty shillings—something I remembered
when I started work in the book trade in 1946 in the
comparative affluence of four pounds a week. Ian had
ended up as manager of a big hotel at Aviemore before
enlisting; he had switched to the paratroops, damaged a
knee and returned to the regiment. The three platoon
commanders were Tommy Fairbairn who had been a
printer; 'Mac' MacGillivray, a saturnine ex-stockbroker;
and Robin Collier who had always intended to join the
regiment, his father being a distinguished Cameron and
a general to boot. Robin was the one officer younger than
I. Attached to us for a month or two we had a lad called
MacLean, destined for the Intelligence Corps, and for a

short time an effervescent Norwegian known for simplicity as Chris.

There had been a lucky vacancy as Company Sergeant Major which I was able to fill by begging for Sgt. Owens from the Carrier Platoon. In all that lay ahead he was a jewel of a CSM, and made just as good a RSM when he was subsequently promoted. Like my first mentor, Sgt. Horbury, he was a Cameron Highlander through and through but not a Scot; he was a Geordie, though years of service had given his Newcassel voice some broad Scots overtones. He was a strong, active man, rather choleric in complexion and manner, absolutely fair in his dealings with his NCOs and the men. Originally a 1st Battalion man, he had been wounded with them in France in 1940.

There were two very good sergeants, Winton and White. The latter had been a miner at Bathgate, near Edinburgh, and had preferred enlistment to the pits: I never came across an ex-miner in the Camerons, or more casually in other regiments, who was not a first class soldier. The junior NCOs were at that time promising rather than good, another change from the old company where long service almost ensured that by the time a man reached the rank of corporal he was bound to be good. But with an excellent CSM and at least two good sergeants, all we needed was a little time: and in turn one could be confident that unless the platoon officers were a disaster, which was far from the case, good NCOs would lead good soldiers.

Unlike my officers, many of the Jocks seemed young, or at least they were my own age, which I enjoyed after being by many years the youngest member of the old C Company. Some were the original territorials from Inverness-shire or the Hebrides, others had volunteered at eighteen in order to join the regiment of their choice, and many of course had been called up as conscripts. Even in those circumstances the old regimental magic had worked, and young men who had been arbitrarily posted to the Camerons were as conscious of the tartan patch on their sleeve or the regimental badge on their balmoral as those who had schemed and pulled strings to get into the regiment. Inevitably there were one or two men who should never have been soldiers at all. A really stupid man needs so much coaxing and shoving that, apart from being a danger to his comrades, he can drive his officer or NCO wild; and that cannot be permitted. One corporal had to be busted because he couldn't learn when he had to be patient and when to be rough.

We had our successes, on the other hand. I remember one man, Kilbride, who had a dismal record and every appearance of instability, not surprising since both his parents had been killed in the savage bombing of Clyde-bank. Instead of writing him off, his platoon commander persevered with him, helped by CSM Owens who had a way with difficult men, despite his fierce appearance. In four months Kilbride turned into a good soldier, indeed he applied for a regular 'seven and five' —seven years with the colours, five years in the reserve.

The army did its best for its conscripts as citizens in arms. Equipped with little pamphlets, we lectured the company every week on current affairs, rather a strain on both parties, I felt, only eased when one let the dis-cussion rip. The Education Officer attached to the battalion was always anxious to help, which usually meant tackling illiteracy. One man was ashamed of not being able to read, and went to extraordinary lengths to conceal it. His technique to find out whether he was on duty was to hang round the notice board and say, 'It's a dom' shame they've put So-and-So on guard two nights running.'

'They havena'.'

'They have so.'

'Ah'm telling you they havena'. Listen ye sumph,' and the names would be reeled off.

'Ach, ye're right.' It was all rather a time-wasting procedure. When he was rumbled, and I told him that reading was a knack like riding a bike, an art I hadn't learned till years after most boys, he got over his shame and took to his lessons. But I failed with another lad, who could just sign his name in his paybook but otherwise was wholly illiterate. He refused any attempt to teach him. His grandfather and his father had both done well in the circus world without being able to read or write a word, and he wasn't going to jeopardize his precious inheritance. 'Ye can jile me, sir, but I winna learn my letters.' Logic won, and he didn't.

Old soldiers and new soldiers are alike in putting up with almost anything pretty cheerfully if they can see an object to it. Barrack life and routine training can easily become pointless, hence boring; and a bored unit is a bad unit. For instance, kit inspections should teach the soldier to look after his gear, since the slovenly man who loses bits and pieces is a menace in action, and the quickest way to see that it is all correct is to have it laid out. To forget the object and concentrate on the means, by insisting for example on socks being folded just so, is to make it pointless, and thus objectionable. Again, there are many reasons for drill, not the least being the sense of cohesion it produces, and the pleasure men feel in performing anything well, but square bashing for the hell of it is a dreary occupation. I believed in exacting a very high standard of drill, but in dismissing the company after five minutes to have some free time. This of course kept the standard high, since we would grind away for a full hour if it wasn't so. CSM Owens was rather scandalized at first: 'What if the RSM or the Adjutant come along and find we're no' drillin'?' But he became so proud of the result that he forgave the unorthodoxy.

A soldier is useless if he cannot get to the right place to handle his weapons effectively, which for any infantryman means using his legs. This was easy in our little camp at Voe with mile upon mile of untenanted moor and bog all round us, and we really took a great deal of exercise. We had to begin modestly by marching along the only road, but then took to the hills until we were doing company schemes which involved twenty and twenty-five miles, much of it over very rough country with plenty of creeping and crawling and some shooting at the end of it. To set up the scheme with the 'enemy' in the right place, and with a minimum of risk from the use of live ammunition, meant covering most of the ground with one or two of the NCOs the previous weekend.

Our camp had a boiler of sorts, so when weapons had been cleaned we could usually run to a hot shower after our outings. It was always followed by a foot inspection and clean socks. Blisters called for rebuke rather than sympathy, and my fuss over toenails became, as I couldn't help overhearing, a company joke. Many of the Jocks were oddly reluctant to cut their toenails unless ordered to do so, and would have preferred to keep a thing like a one-inch chisel gouging through their socks into the toe of their boot, and crippling them on a serious march. Every platoon had to have a pair of nail scissors, and they had to be used. I cannot remember in the desert ever looking at 15 Platoon's feet, perhaps assuming that old soldiers knew better than I how important their feet were; certainly they marched splendidly, and I was determined that the new C Company would march just as well.

We always wound up our week's exercise with a booted run on Saturday morning, and of course football in the afternoon as well as at any odd moment during the week. The fact that we were fit enough to cover the ground and do our little exercises without distress was a self-evident object to all this activity.

The real sweat was doing the same thing, though over fewer miles, at night. Road marching is a desperate affair in the dark, one always nods off at the halts, while going cross country on a moonless night meant falling into one peat hag after another. We got back looking as though we had been dipped in cocoa. Even so there were compensations in some magnificent displays of the Northern Lights, or the Merry Dancers as they are called in Shetland, most aptly since the shifting radiance looks very like a twirling array of lilac and green and pink crinolines dipping and swaying round a celestial ballroom.

Our amusements were largely of our own making, although we were visited by an occasional concert party, and we ran a weekly truck into Lerwick for the flicks. Sometimes a guest night took one or two of the officers into the battalion mess where we usually ended up playing room rugger at which our Norwegian and naval guests were better than dancing reels. I remember a return visit to drink gins in a submarine. The way inside was a small hole with a vertical ladder, down which my companion clambered. He steadily sank from view while his kilt remained on deck until it too disappeared, round his ears. There were some very surprised sailors down below.

We had a tiny mess at Voe, the boarded-off end of a Nissen hut, where we spent most of our off-duty hours in discussion and chop-logic argument. We won the war, of course, in half a dozen ways but found fullest scope in settling the sort of country we wanted afterwards. On this our only argument was that it should be different, and better, but how and to what degree we found as hard to determine as the politicians have done ever since. We weren't wholly Utopian because most of the others had seen enough of life as it is to temper my wilder flights of radicalism as well as add weight to the argument for change. Mac, the stockbroker, had our eyes popping in amazement at the sums of money involved in various City deals, and at some of the dubious transactions he had observed; Tommy had industrial experience on which he commented coolly and sensibly; while Ian Jack alternatively horrified us and doubled us up in laughter at his stories of hotel life above and below stairs. He talked well, with passion and wit. It was like having *The Road to Wigan Pier* and a Firbank novel within the same covers.

I was lucky in having a very good batman; an officer ought to be so immersed in his work as to have no time to bother about his own small comforts. Finn was a treasure. First of all, he was a good soldier with some service. He was a good driver in any conditions including shellfire, and he was a brave and intelligent runner when messages had to be delivered verbally. That lay in the future; for the present he was neat himself, and kept all my belongings tidy and mended, and he dished up our cookhouse grub in the tiny mess with elegance. He was fair headed, always rather pale, given to blushing particularly when he was about to make a joke, much admired in the company for his skill as a footballer and in constant demand as our only fully trained barber; he had been a hairdresser in Peterhead before he enlisted.

We took pains to be on good terms with our few neighbours. The doctor had been in Shetland for thirty-five years. His wife told me that when he began to practise his payment from most patients was a string of fish or a bag of potatoes, 'Yet we got by, and have never been aught but happy.' There was an old widow, a great pipe smoker, with a flow of language that jolted even the hardest Jocks; her son was an M.A. from Edinburgh. The little mill employed fifteen or twenty people, very hospitable to us in their cottages at tea-time on a Sunday, the women knitting non-stop and at prodigious speed. Just before I left New York, I had blued the last of my advances of pay in buying at Saks Fifth Avenue some twinset jerseys for my mother and sister; it was ironic to find them being made at Voe for export to Saks. The owner of the mill, a Mr. Adie, had known Louise's uncle Frank Morley when he was in Voe to examine the last whaling station in Britain.

This was a tenuous but comforting link, for in September 1943 Louise and I were married, with David Douglas as my best man. She had been posted to the U.S. Embassy in London, to work in the Office of War Information; there ensued some heart-searching letters, and a burst of telegrams which came through the military system, so that the company was well informed of proceedings, although too well-mannered to let me in on the book which was made on the result. Leave, a special licence, and then three days of honeymoon; Grosvenor Square seemed a long way from Voe, so even an avuncular connection was better than none at all. My gloom at returning was lifted by the company, who treated my wedding as an occasion for public rejoicing, specially those whose bets had come up, and by Finn who gave me an exquisitely-knitted pair of local gloves 'for the mustress'. To the very newly married, what a glow follows the recognition that one has acquired a mistress—*anglice*, a missus.

One way and another, C Company was in good shape when the battalion at last had orders to move, in October. The officers were working hard, Ian and Robin Collier in particular showing real leadership, the NCOs were steady and the men were smart on parade, in really good physical condition and above all cheerful. One learned to judge corporate spirit by all that went on off-duty; the sort of shouting at a football match or the type of chaffing and banter in the cookhouse queue, even the tone of the laughter, were indicative of how the company was feeling.

We sailed from Lerwick on November 3rd and fetched up at Bridge of Allan in Stirlingshire to prepare for embarkation overseas. There was the usual proliferation of rumours about our destination, the front runners being India for the Burma campaign, where the 1st Battalion was serving, or the Med for the Italian front. There was no time to spare for speculation: the men had to be sent off on leave in big batches, kit had to be made up, all ammunition checked by Ordnance, weapons inspected by the armourers, vehicles overhauled or replaced. I took the opportunity of clearing out the Company Office. It was surprising how much printed matter the army showered on one. Some of it was important, but some was clearly generated by branches of the staff who had to justify their establishment—a medical pamphlet, for instance, which informed one that 'injuries caused by leopard or tiger bites should be treated as for cat or dog bites.'

A few men could not go abroad, often because they were too young. One keen young soldier turned out, when we finally got his birth certificate, to be only sixteen. They had to be posted away to other units, and in turn we had to absorb a large draft from the Liverpool Scottish, one of the regiment's affiliated territorial units. It was not good, though probably unavoidable, to make up a battalion to full strength just before going abroad, since it was too bewildering for the new arrival. He was sent off to a company where the Quartermaster Sergeant pounced on him to check his paybook, with its allowances and stoppages, and to issue kit. The Sergeant Major 'documented' him to make sure we had all his particulars accurately recorded, from his army number to his next of kin, and his platoon commander interviewed him, allotted him to a section and made sure he knew his section commander and platoon sergeant. It was even more muddling for this draft because most of the company was away on embarkation leave. Owens and I agreed that some of our intake looked promising, some the reverse, but that we would soon have the latter up to company standard—the usual litany.

Amongst the new arrivals was a German boy who had left Breslau in 1938, and spent three years working in a clothing factory in Leeds. His nationality was doubtful, and I put it to him as tactfully as I could that he might be in a dangerous situation if he were captured, and that in any case he could well be shooting at his own kith and kin, though I suppose most of them had been exterminated. 'That would suit me fine,' he replied with a broad smile, and indeed it did; Fairfax, for that was the name he had chosen, was to prove an excellent soldier and NCO in Italy.

Ian Jack came back from his leave, and I whizzed off to spend what seemed the very brief fourteen days of my embarkation leave. It was as well that Louise and I did not know when we parted that our next meeting would be in two and a half years' time, in April 1946. Back to the battalion a week before our deadline, to find that C Company was six over strength and that I had to decide who should stay behind. One of the new draft settled his future by putting a bullet through his foot, most incompetently since he blew most of his ankle off in the process; which meant recording all the necessary evidence to be left behind for his eventual court martial. Who else should stay was difficult. Good soldiers whose wife was about to have a baby, or with a mother on the edge of death? Or some of the newcomers who seemed unstable and might be nothing but a liability? Or even Pte. Mac-Ewen whose new teeth might or might not be ready by embarkation day? I smoked furiously for an hour, but inevitably kept the good men and let the doubtful ones go. Virtue has to be its own reward in wartime. The good soldier like the willing horse had to get what satisfaction he could from carrying an extra burden.

One could not alter this basic unfairness, although within its limits one had to take the greatest pains to be fair. To keep one man and release another when each had roughly the same compassionate grounds for exemption from active service abroad would have been, at my level, an unfair way of dealing with individuals. As it was, my decisions caused some heart-breaking disappointments but no grievances.

We embarked on December 17th. Unlike my false start in 1940, this time we could sail straight through the

Mediterranean rather than round the whole of Africa to reach Egypt. We landed at Port Said on Hogmanay, two years after a previous failure to celebrate the same occasion on our way from the desert to the Sudan, and moved to camp at Mena, just outside Cairo.

We had two possible destinations. One was the Mountain Warfare School in Lebanon, to which we actually sent an advance party, while the other was to rejoin the 11th Indian Infantry Brigade in Italy, and serve once more with the red eagle badge of the 4th Indian Division. When we knew it was to be the latter, I felt the wheel had finally come round full circle. Off we went on January 19th 1944, landing on the 25th at Taranto; it was good to set foot on continental soil again, despite the stories of Beirut's attractions told by the abortive advance party. I was delighted to find the Rajputana Rifles still in the brigade; our third battalion was the 2nd/7th Gurkhas, who were to become good friends. The other two brigades in the division were already getting into position at Cassino, and 11th Brigade was to follow. Training was over.

7

CASSINO

WE had a week in camp at Taranto before moving up, which was valuable to shake the company together. It gave us a chance to use our legs, and to test our ability to make ourselves comfortable, a vital art for the soldier. The seasoned campaigner can mitigate the most miserable conditions with ingenuity and common sense, and it makes a lot of difference to his performance. It was also a chance to give the company cooks a workout in easy circumstances.

I had found one great improvement in coming back to regimental service, the fact that the army had formed a Catering Corps which taught men how to cook. In C Company we were particularly fortunate in Corporal Ball, who was to demonstrate his ability, with his cooks, to produce palatable food in all circumstances, mud, rain, snow or heat wave. We fed the brigadier one day (no longer Reggie Savory, now commanding a division, but Brigadier V. C. Griffin); he was highly struck by Ball's skill in topping up a good dinner for 120 people with pancakes and syrup, from one petrol burner. Ball was at least half gypsy, from the north of England. A precursor of Yul Brynner, he kept his head shaved which he claimed in truth was a cleanly habit, and he wore little gold rings in his ears. We managed as a unit to hang on to enough kilts to equip at least NCOs when they went on leave; later on, Cpl. Ball argued that, after all we had gone through, he was far more a Cameron Highlander than a member of the Army Catering Corps, so I found him a kilt. With his gleaming billiard ball of a pate and his ear-rings he was a strange sight in it, but Ball had the physique of a heavyweight and it would have been a brave man in the leave camp who smiled at his appearance.

Before leaving Egypt we had been ordered to provide a
draft for the Argylls, so the last two or three misfits had
left the company. I felt bold enough to push the whole lot
off into the town one evening; they had some fun, drank
and didn't like their first vino, and all turned up back in
camp on time, which pleased me. The NCOs were un-
changed from Shetland, as were the officers with one addition, Andy Anderson who had been in the Argentine before
the war and like Mac of the Stock Exchange was as fervid
a Scot as most emigrés are. The company officers were a
hard-working lot, and a very entertaining bunch when we
sat round our hurricane lamp in the evening.

On February 2nd we moved up in cattle trucks on the
railway past Salerno and Naples to Capua; not for us
Hannibal's luxurious winter quarters there, for we transferred to lorries and joined the brigade at Pietramellara, a
half-ruined but still inhabited village. It was here I
realized with a jolt that this was a different kind of war,
one which involved civilians. In the desert and in Eritrea,
the fighting went on without damaging anyone but
soldiers, all the battles were in terrain that nobody had
tried to inhabit: war was idiocy, but it was self-contained.
But here were poor folk whose houses had been smashed,
their belongings destroyed, fields unsown and animals
killed; every family had suffered death and injury, the
children were in rags and evidently half starving. War
wasn't merely idiotic, it was wicked and cruel. The sight
of the children especially shocked us. 'I dinna' care about
the Eyeties, they probably thought Musso great, but they
kids make me grue,' said Sgt. White, echoing the general
opinion; and the cookhouse gave most of them at least one
square meal a day. Alas, the shock wore off as we pro-
gressed through Italy and the squalor, the waste and the
misery deepened.

We spent an uncomfortable week in deep mud, the rain
almost unceasing and the gunfire at Cassino as a continuous
background. 'You'd think,' I wrote to Louise, 'a Jock

who'd been flooded in the night and hadn't a dry stitch of clothing would be miserable in the morning, trying to light a fire in six inches of mud with a steady drizzle coming down — but not a bit, they were full of beans'; and

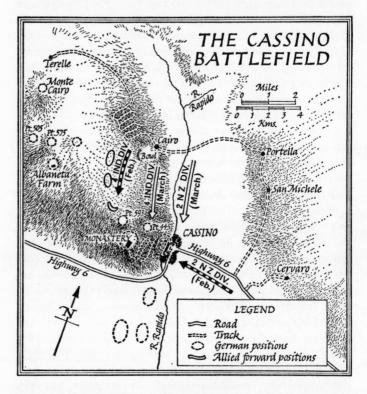

a couple of days later after forty more hours of rain I could tell her the Jocks were singing.

The Camerons were handicapped by the fact that none of our transport had arrived yet from Alex, and so our equipment and weapons consisted of what we could carry. In the circumstances it was not surprising that C and D Companies were ordered up to Cassino for portering duties, although it was bad luck for the battalion to be

CASSINO

committed piecemeal instead of as a unit. The C.O.'s behaviour was a problem. He had become increasingly
agitated as we moved nearer to action, which was certainly nothing to do with his own safety, but perhaps because he couldn't bear to see his battalion fulfilling the
purposes for which it had been trained; like a housewife
with a brand-new duster who would sooner keep it tidily
folded in a drawer than see it soiled with use. His concern
became ludicrous and embarrassing when the two companies set off in M.T. at 1 in the morning, a simple
operation which he clucked and fussed over. It was a relief
to get away, even though the drive down the main road
was frightening, at full speed and with no lights since it
was under German observation. We de-bussed at 4 a.m.
and marched through the mud to a deep valley at Portella
where we found 5th Brigade. They were being supplied by
jeep, but would need men as well as mules when they went
up the hill.

The supply lines of most of the Allied forces were tangled
up in that valley, Indians, New Zealanders, some French,
the Poles and of course the Americans whose assault on
Cassino was just drawing to a fruitless close. In the jumble
I found a jeep and trailer which appeared to have no
owner, so I made off with it, to Owens's horror who saw
himself giving evidence at my court martial. Finn took
over the jeep and I rejoiced in having some transport for
our cookhouse gear—prematurely, for it was stolen back
next day. We had nothing to do, so the Jocks busied themselves in making new friends and in swapping rations. The
G.I.s' ration box was a source of fascinated wonder, in
particular the bouillon powder. 'Hey, Wullie, whit's this
balloon powder for?' a question followed by a string of
mountingly rabelaisian suggestions.

Our valley was a side cleft in the main valley of the
Rapido river. Across it lay the town of Cassino, with an
old castle on a spur above; behind and beyond towered
the snow-topped ridges rising to Monte Cairo. Crowning

the main ridge over the town was the monastery, its many storeys looking as if they had grown organically from the grey rock in which they were founded. The bronze roof picked up a dull gleam from the pale winter sun. It fell just short of beauty, but its position and mass made it enormously impressive, with a commanding outlook over the entire valley and over every approach to Cassino. Farther north, the Allies had landed a force at Anzio, on January 22nd, to turn the German flank. Far from incommoding the enemy, the Anzio beachhead was critically close to disaster. The Allies had to force their way north to relieve it and, it was hoped, link up with the forces there to achieve the capture of Rome. There were only two roads to Rome, the coastal road with countless bridges over marshlands, and Highway 6, further inland and plugged as effectively by Cassino as the Via Imperiale in Eritrea had been by Keren. The Adriatic front could bring no pressure to bear owing to the almost total lack of east–west roads: so the thinking was that Cassino must be forced at all costs. Since it was firmly believed that the Germans were occupying and observing from the monastery, that became one of the costs. It was appalling to watch flight after flight of heavy bombers unloading over it. Huge clouds of dust and smoke cleared to reveal a shattered hulk of masonry. Never mind the Germans, one thought, what about the monks, and what about the priceless library, and the smashed splendour of the building? We found later that the only military effect of the bombing was to make the ruin virtually impregnable, with a vast *glacis* of broken stone to protect it. It remained a perfect observation post.

The day after the bombing, I was ordered by 5th Brigade to take C Company across the main valley to the village of Cairo, tucked into the wild tangle of hills beyond the monastery. We crossed the low ground fast, in very open order, without casualties although the shelling was fairly heavy. The job was to carry ammunition up that night to the forward troops of the brigade who had relieved the Americans on the ground they had won. The division was very impressed by the courage and bearing of the G.I.s, who had suffered severe losses in their attacks, and then sat tight against all counter attacks where they had been brought to a halt. Many of them had refused to be evacuated as casualties despite wounds and trench foot, and had to be lifted out of their cramped foxholes when the time came for relief.

C Company's portering was heavy work, just like Keren with the addition of mud underfoot and sleet down the neck. We had a couple of hours' rest at dawn and then repeated the performance. When we got back to the ammo dump at noon I was told to take the company over to the 4th/6th Rajputana Rifles, now up the hill and due to attack that night a crest known as Point 593 where the Germans had twice beaten back attacks by the Royal Sussex.

I left the company to have some rest, and climbed up the hill with Finn to the Raj Rif HQ to find out what we had to do. Their C.O., Lt. Col. Scott, wanted us to follow the leading companies with loads of extra grenades and ammunition—essential, since the ground was so steep that a soldier couldn't put in an assault weighed down with additional burdens, and the risk of being pushed off an objective by a counter attack was very high unless supplies could be replenished at once. But it was a beastly job. The company arrived under Ian after dark, and had to be allotted in parties to the Raj Rif companies and their loads sorted out. Zero hour, unimaginatively, was midnight, the attack going in immediately after an intense barrage. The Germans put up flares, unusually short-lived, so that one saw the battlefield in a series of brilliant flashes, the smoke and dust from the shell-bursts foaming up in red-tinged clouds. The sepoys went like tiger cats but the hillside, the barbed wire and fierce defensive fire were too much for them. There were many casualties, but nothing achieved. It was typical of this hopelessly dis-organized battle that through no fault of the army, the divisional attack could not be synchronized with the bombing of the monastery; it would have given the un-fortunate infantry a sporting chance. Instead, the forward troops had suffered casualties from the bombs because their brigadier had been given less than fifteen minutes' warning that the monastery was to be pulverized.

Cassino was our first experience of an 'allied' battle and we did not like it. We could and did respect our fellow soldiers of all nationalities, but the command structure and staff work seemed to us below par. There was sardonic amusement at the story that some of the bombers had been so inaccurately navigated that they had dropped their load on the headquarters of the American commander of the Cassino battle, General Mark Clark.

I could hardly believe our luck when I found we had only suffered two wounded, though very concerned that Finn was missing; he had got separated in the confusion as I moved from one carrying party to another. He turned up soon after first light, and in my relief at seeing him again I rated him soundly for getting lost. It was only later I learned, and from Owens not him, that he thought I had been hit, and had been looking for me. For most of the men, it was an introduction to the noise and confusion of a night action and they behaved well. Discipline remained good throughout, always a factor in keeping casualties down. Daylight showed that the Raj Rif would not want porters for a while, they had suffered 196 casualties, so I took the company back to a deep quarry near Cairo vil-lage where I had left the cooks and the CQMS. It was shelled now and again, but only casually, and we could rest. After thirty-six hours of carrying heavy loads up 2,000 feet of steep and rocky mountain, we were ex-hausted. We were relieved by A Company a few days later, which gave us a chance to wash and shave. Un-fortunately A's take-over must have been observed by a

German F.O.O., for the quarry was registered and then bombarded by a heavy mortar battery, killing eight men and wounding fourteen.

On February 24th the battalion at last began to function as a unit, with orders to move into Sector Reserve, in the same tangle of foothills. I always enjoyed having the company 'on detachment' but to be under command of another unit was by no means the same thing. It was a pleasure to receive orders from the normal source, one's own battalion, and to be linked up again in the usual signal network; good, also to be able to rely on our own Quartermaster for admin back-up.

It was a trying move in the dark to the Bowl, a Devil's Punch Bowl lined with rock instead of turf; all our kit was loaded on refractory mules which kicked off some rations and cookhouse equipment. Here we spent a week in the rain and sleet, occasionally shelled and once shot up by a German fighter, standing-by to counter attack a threatened enemy penetration which never materialized. It was an unhappy week, since we could get no clear picture of how the battle was going and it was impossible therefore to explain the position to the Jocks; and puzzled or bewildered men can't be effective soldiers. In the Bowl we had a delivery of 'comforts'—jerseys, gloves, mufflers and the first string vest any of us had seen. I had the company draw lots, the officers taking what was left. Nobody wanted the string vest, but I found myself very glad of it. Our outfit consisted of battledress, of course, the trouser ends tucked between two pairs of socks with ankle gaiters over them; a scarf, sleeveless leather jerkin, mittens or gloves (I had prudently brought an old pair of ski mitts), a woollen cap or tin hat depending on circumstances, and a ground sheet worn over all to keep out some of the rain and snow.

Corporal Ball and his cooks carried on imperturbably; on one occasion on the other side of the valley he had produced a truly delicious cauliflower *au gratin* when the rations had included a supply of vegetables. His gypsy background produced some qualms however. Horse meat, he always claimed, if properly treated was better than beef, the secret being to pound it for twenty minutes on your doorstep before braising it. To prove his point he went leaping down the hillside when a mule was killed by

ITALY:
TARANTO TO THE RUBICON

LEGEND
Gothic Line
Gustav Line

shellfire, waving his cleaver, and returned with a dozen fresh steaks to the shuddering horror of the company. I made Ian join me in eating several of them, telling him it would be invaluable experience for his return to post-war hotel keeping. Ball was almost right, for the meat was excellent, if a little sweet without benefit, of sauce, and certainly more palatable than camel or goat. 'And that's only

CASSINO: The Monastery before . . .

. . . and after the bombardment

CASSINO: Part of the battlefield. Point 593 lies on the right of
the ruined Monastery

The Pipes and Drums at San Marino

army mule, sir; now if ever we come across a nice horse . . .'

There were no lights of course, and after dark the company kipped down by sections and platoons in two-man bivouac tents. Between rounds of the company to talk with their men, the off-duty officers would cram into my bivvy to continue the discussions we had had in Shetland. From a letter home, I see that we spent hours one night discussing post-war education, the creation of national parks in Scotland and the best ways of drinking rum. By now we had lost MacGillivray with acute ear trouble; he had been badly blown up in the London blitz, and the noise and the cold of Cassino had done his eardrums no good.

It was almost a relief on March 2nd to be ordered up to the slopes of Point 593 to relieve 7th Brigade. C Company took over from a company of the 1st/2nd Gurkhas during a heavy fall of snow and mortar bombs, one of the latter killing Pte. MacMahon, a good soldier. Point 593 was a minor crest on a long ridge running up to the monastery, some hundreds of yards away. The crest itself had been held by the Germans against all attacks so far, and our positions were dug in the slope leading up to it, more or less where the attacks had petered out. Since we were on the forward slope, every movement in daylight was observed and brought down instant fire from snipers and mortars. The only reason for retaining the position was, I suppose, to have a forming-up place for yet another night attack. The section posts were part sangar, part dugout, each holding four or five men. In daytime we had to stay put, peering at the German positions seventy-five yards away, getting cramp in our legs, watching the snow drifting in, and twitching when the mortar bombs came down.

It was a bad position for pretty raw troops, because it was too inactive and because the sections were so isolated in daytime. This put a heavy strain on the section commanders, an unfair one because they were not old soldiers and needed the back-up of their officer or at least of a senior NCO. I tried to put myself in the mind of the Jocks, pinned down in their wretched positions all day with hardly a chance of anything so positive as a shot at a German, their leadership dependent on their young lance-corporal or corporal, and concluded that I would feel very forlorn. The conclusion led to no remedy, but to continued admiration that somehow they were sticking it. Military discipline, which of course doesn't just consist of rules about 'short back and sides', was both total and, in a curious way, self-imposed. Saki somewhere makes a nincompoop Secretary of War back out of an awkward situation with the epigram, 'Discipline to be effective must be optional'. There is more wisdom in it than Saki intended, because cowed, unthinking obedience quite unfits a soldier for the modern battlefield. The centurion in the New Testament had the root of the matter when he explained, 'I say to this man, Go, and he goeth; and to another, Come, and he cometh': the reason he gives is, 'For I am a man *under* authority.' The shared acceptance of a common rule by the leader and the led is the bedrock of true discipline.

Officers should be in amongst their men, but the platoon commanders had to hole up in their command posts and could only get round their sections after dark, not the best way of keeping spirits up. I was in like case, sharing a hole with the CSM; the signaller and his set were in an adjoining hole. There was nothing much to do in daytime but to chat, and after three weeks of this troglodyte life Owens and I knew each other even better. Occasionally he won some cigarettes off me playing solo, and part of the time we passed in cooking and slowly eating our grub. Each post cooked its own food over an old tin with holes punched in the side and an inch of petrol in the bottom — our old brew-up system in the desert. It made an effective stove, and our rations were good unless the nightly mule train had copped a burst of shelling. I noted with pride one day that Owens and I had cooked a breakfast of coffee and bacon and beans, with fried bread, on our ex-condensed milk tin.

Night time was when we were active, rotating platoons and sections, waiting for the mules to come up with the rations and take down the wounded. It was not possible to shift the companies about as Andy had done at Keren, but at least I could ring the changes with the three platoons, two forward and one back. We had a couple of little wireless sets to give some communication between each platoon and its forward sections, and a telephone line, constantly cut by shells and mortar bombs and repaired every night, from the platoons back to me. Ian, with one of the forward platoons, rang up in great excitement to say that his wireless set had with luck and some fiddling tuned into the German wavelength, and that he had Fairfax, our German Jock, listening in: now for some first-hand information on what the enemy was planning to do! An hour later he came through again, amid gusts of his unmistakeable laughter, that what they'd got was a German forces broadcast, and that all the hot news he could tell me was what the Jerries claimed to be doing in the Dneiper Bend. It was the only occasion anybody laughed on that phone.

I had communications problems with battalion HQ, but they were physical ones and no longer connected with the presence of the C.O. who had been taken off to hospital, a very sick man, and replaced by the Second-in-Command. Gordon Munro had been an Inverness lawyer and a territorial of long service, and he commanded us with great skill through what could easily have been a bad patch. As well as a vast black moustache and a balmoral of a curious mildewy green tinge, Gordon possessed a command of Latin which he was convinced I shared. When he was on the air in clear to C Company, he would break into it, baffling the Germans no doubt as deeply as me. It was, I told him later, his barbarous legal Latin and his old pronunciation to blame rather than my shaky classics. I could record one success however when he had to warn me urgently of the threat of a weapon new to us: I was rather pleased to have translated *dracones* correctly as flame-throwers, though even more pleased when the threat never came to anything.

While we in theory neutralized the monastery, the main battle continued with a series of assaults on Cassino town and the castle above it. The savage fighting won no ground, and the bombers came in again to blast the town, a mile and a half from our positions and away down in the valley. Our hilltop shook as the bombs exploded, and even at that distance we were shrouded in dust and smoke. The result was another failure, the town was reduced to such a mass of rubble that the New Zealand tanks couldn't get through it.

After a couple of weeks, with nothing to show for the steady trickle of casualties, the company was down in the mouth and it wasn't easy to jolly the men along as one stumped round the positions at night. We were short of officers, too. Ian was badly wounded in the thigh, Robin Collier wounded also, while Tommy Fairbairn went down with acute dysentery. Anderson and I were very glad when Bill Garroch from the 5th Battalion arrived; what a place though to join a company and take over a platoon. The strain showed in various ways, from villainous bad temper to excessive jumpiness. One night one of the Jocks near me, Pte. Glaney, had an hysterical fit; he had reached his personal breaking point. I gentled him like a horse until he could listen and then was rough with him; surely he was man enough to stick it like the others, however bloody things were, instead of screeching like a schoolgirl? He took a few deep, shuddering breaths and said, 'Right you are, sir, I'll thole it', and did so; he was killed the next night. That was a death that really lay on my mind. If we had not been so thin on the ground, and I had sent him down the hill as a shell-shock case, would he have survived to see his wife again? Would another man have been killed in his place, or would that mortar bomb have exploded harmlessly?

As I lay curled up in my hole the following day asking these and many other questions of myself, the allied artillery opened up on us. It was far worse than Keren because there were far more guns, and for twenty minutes before the shoot could be stopped we were sick with fear. It was an intensely heavy bombardment, but surprisingly the shells only wounded eight men in the company, though they created a slump in morale; at least poor Glaney had been killed by the enemy. The episode confirmed my belief that heavy mortars were far more punishing in mountain warfare than either side's shellfire, a belief that wasn't much comfort since the Germans owned the mortars.

It was with thankfulness that after three weeks we handed over the positions on 593 to the same Gurkhas. We had had thirty-five casualties, D Company nearly sixty, to no very apparent purpose, but I suppose everyone's thought as we stumbled down to the Bowl was 'At least I'm in one piece'. Once there, we tried to sort ourselves out in readiness for a brigade move back into rest; it was the first time I had seen any of the company in daylight, except Owens two feet away, since we had left the Bowl. We boiled lots of water and had a shave. My own beard looked splendid in the shaving mirror, too good to lose without a pang; then I washed my face and was left with a pale, barely visible fuzz. Off with it, quick. I remember we had news there of a coal strike at home, which generated caustic comments from the Jocks, in particular those who had been in the pits.

Our move on March 25th was pandemonium. At midnight the Bowl was crammed with three battalions and 250 mules, but it happened to be one of the few nights when the enemy didn't shoot it up. The battalion's allocation of mules had to be distributed to the companies, followed by the task of lashing our heavy gear to the packsaddles, the weight equalized so that the load would balance, and not end up under the mule's belly. To do all this in tar-barrel darkness and pouring rain, and in a fever to get out before the shelling started, was a nightmare. Even so, I was pleased that the company was functioning properly despite the conditions; officers and NCOS were commanding their men by giving orders, and not by shouting and cursing, except of course at the mules. Once down at the foot of the hill, we streaked across the valley by companies to Portella and then on to San Michele. It was only eight miles or so, but after three weeks in our little holes it was a wearying march and we were thankful to crawl into lorries which took us back to Venafro. We ate a large breakfast, and slept the clock round.

The first step was to get clean. We went in squads to a mobile bath unit and had an issue of kit afterwards. The feel of a clean shirt was wonderful, the one I had been wearing day and night for six weeks was so filthy that I told Finn to burn it. The next thing was to check all company stores and indent for replacements for lost or damaged items; it was good to find that whatever we had lost, we still had all our weapons, and in good order. The third was to get hold of some beer and let everybody unwind. That process was much helped when Gordon Munro held a battalion memorial service for those killed at Cassino—fifty-one, with 150 wounded. The brigadier made a point of attending, and gave us a pat on the back; the padre offered some simple and good prayers, and to sing the 'Auld Hundredth' with four hundred others was a powerful experience. But the backbone of the service was 'The Flowers of the Forest' played by a single piper, and of course the gut-churning notes of the Last Post and Reveille. It let off a strong head of emotional steam, which I found particularly helpful after spending hours writing letters to the relations of those killed.

There was always a great deal of administration to catch up with when we came out of the line. The Company

Office, a tin uniform trunk, was one of the first things to appear from B Echelon. Casualties had to be properly documented and the adjutant informed, and the personal belongings of the dead packed up to be sent to their family, which always made me swallow hard. I used to go through a man's things to make sure nothing would be sent home which could cause pain. With Owens and the platoon commanders I had to fill vacancies among the NCOs and if necessary reorganize the men in sections and platoons. The CQMS's turn came next—the revised ration strength of the company, replacement kit, the imprest account if a pay day were in the offing. Then there would be the soldiers' own requests to attend to, such as a change in the allotment of pay to wife or mother, or some worry about affairs at home which had to be referred to the army welfare people. The Company Office in its figurative sense, not just the tin box, is also the tribunal of justice for all minor offences, but in Italy I seldom had to sit in judgement; soldiers don't get into trouble on active service.

In fact, the Camerons had not done much at Cassino except be there; our casualties were lighter than those in other battalions of the division who had been fiercely involved in attack and counter-attack. It was a bad battle to open the account of a new unit, for it was too big and muddled to let one grasp what was going on. If our M.T. and heavy weapons had arrived in time for us to act as a battalion rather than be committed in dribs and drabs, and if Gordon had been in command from our landing at Taranto, I believe it would not have been so depressing an action.

To the historian, battles are important if they produce a radical shift in the pattern of war, and they are big if large numbers of troops are involved. To the ordinary soldier the result is certainly important—have we won or lost?— though he tends to think first of the immediate result in his own sector: but whether he is involved in a 'big' battle is immaterial. He can only do what he can, for as long as he can, in a skirmish or a major set-piece, and the extent of his capacity and the style in which he exerts it depend on his training and morale. Sidi Barrani was a walkover, Keren or Cassino bitterly fought slogging matches, yet Pte. Crowe was just as dead from a casual potshot in the first as the dozens killed in sustained bombardment in the others.

8

GOTHIC LINE

WHEN we moved again at the beginning of April beyond Benevento C Company was picking up. Cleanliness is followed by smartness and in turn by self-respect. A judicious modicum of parades and some exercise in the sun instead of the rain did wonders; the warmth was revitalizing. The fields around us were full of activity, whole families out hoeing and pruning, with an occasional ox-team dragging a heavy plough. I got some of the men off on a forty-eight hour leave to a rest camp, and with the remainder I put on a party one night for D Company, i.e. we clubbed our beer ration and had a sing-song.

We were near a small village, more or less undamaged. The people still had a roof over their heads, the children weren't starving, spring had arrived and they were cheerful, which cheered us up too. Finn bought a bag of charcoal to try out a home-made brazier, as well as a few eggs which were a rare delicacy. He set me up in a little straw hut in the middle of a field, a granary I suppose, and full of field mice. As always when conditions permitted, he put a box beside my sleeping bag as a bedside table, with a candle or hurricane lamp on it, Louise's photograph and whatever books were in my valise. Verse stayed the course better than prose, and the minimum travelling library consisted of two little volumes of Coleridge and one of Burns. It was very pleasant in the granary after dark, the mice pattering through the straw roof in indignation at my trespass. Lights Out is always sounded in a Highland regiment by a slow march played by a single piper round the company area; one would overhear a drowsy conversation outside over a last fag, someone

125

grunting as he fell asleep, and then silence broken only by the sigh of the charcoal settling in the brazier.

By now it was admitted that our battles for Cassino had achieved nothing, which was depressing. Its defence by the Germans was one of the outstanding feats of arms in the war. It eventually fell in May to a concerted attack by both the Fifth and Eighth Armies, the latter being brought across Italy from the Adriatic front by the C. in C., General Alexander. By then the mud had dried up, the rivers had dropped and the assault could be mounted on a twenty-mile front instead of being concentrated on the funnel of Cassino. Two Polish divisions had the task of seizing Monte Cassino and Monastery Hill, which they accomplished from Point 593 with cold-blooded determination and fearful losses. It was the hinge of the enemy position, which then crumbled as the two Allied armies ground forward and the forces in the Anzio beach-head broke out to assail the German flank and rear. If General Mark Clark's personal vanity had not induced him to disobey Alexander's order, by streaking off to make sure his forces were first in Rome instead of closing the trap on the German Tenth Army, we would have been saved much of what lay ahead of us.*

It is as well not to foresee the future. All we knew at the time, with great relief, was that the division was to be shifted across Italy to the Eighth Army front.

In the meantime I took a day off with Ambrose Todd, who commanded D Company, to drive south to Caserta and make a tour of the hospitals around it. Finn drove us in my jeep for a couple of hours through lovely country-side and over appalling roads. I saw two C Company men, Graham and MacKenzie, who had nearly re-covered from their wounds, and CQMS Young, about to be sent home with a badly shattered arm. In the third hospital that we visited I was stunned to be told that Ian

---

* Fred Majdalany's *Cassino* (Longman, 1957) is one of the best descriptions of a protracted battle I have read.

Jack had died there a fortnight earlier. His wound was serious, but I never dreamed it would be fatal, and I had been counting on finding him and having one of our usual uproarious laughing fits. His wife, I knew, was to have another baby in June. Bloody bloody war, and another of the best men gone. I missed Ian as a friend and as an officer every single day of the campaign.

I was very low when we got back late to the camp, to find that I was to join an advance party in the morning as a preliminary to the battalion's next move. I handed over everything to Mac, now re-joined from hospital and who was to bring the company on in due course, and set out with the party, Finn and our kit in the jeep. We did 180 miles over bad mountain roads across the spine of Italy, catching our first sight of the Adriatic at Termoli, and camping at a village called Treglio. The landscape was a delight, with the snow at last disappearing from the hills. The orchards round every village and township were frothing in blossom, so frivolous a sight that one felt censorious as well as uplifted. Since the ration-carrying element of the advance party had got lost, I blessed Finn's prudence in packing a huge wodge of doorstep sandwiches; we munched them in the dark, listening to the gunfire ahead. Next day we moved up to Castel-frentano to take over billets from the Royal Fusiliers, which reminded me of Keren; the resemblance extended to the state of the quarters. It was a charming little town dominated by its cathedral, and with a lively populace who seemed unperturbed by the shelling. Everybody dived into the cellars when the enemy guns opened fire and waited for the sixth shell to burst, which was reckoned to be the normal ration.

There was nothing much to do, after being shown round the positions, during the two days before the battalion came up. The easing of strain was very noticeable, and made me realize what a constant responsibility the care of the company was. I appear from my letters to have unwound by arguing. Whether I was forever disputatious I don't know, possibly a good discussion was something one could safely write home about. That evening I argued about economics and totalitarianism with Gordon, according to a letter to Louise, followed by another hour in the moonlight on Thucydides and the Peloponnesian War with Angus MacKintosh, our adjutant, who was to marry my sister after the war. Good Friday offered no chance of going to church, for I was working out with Sgt. Winton who was to go where, so that he could guide the company directly to their billets. The battalion arrived on Saturday, C Company's impedimenta including four hens which Owens assured me had been purchased and not liberated; and with it arrived the mail — only the second batch received from home since we had left Scotland. By tea-time on Easter Sunday, after a day's scrubbing, the billets were clean if damp, and we could relax under a roof for the first time since we had left Bridge of Allan in December. There was even time to go to the evening mass in the cathedral next door which in those pre-ecumenical days seemed a rather dashing thing to do. Later I sat in my room under a dim light — but *electric* light! — and read my mail and wrote letters, thankful we weren't out in the rain which had started again, and listening to the hours chimed on a cracked bell.

We depended very much on mail from home, and spirits always rose after a good batch caught up with the battalion. To send letters back presented some problems, and not just the physical one of seizing an opportunity to write. All the soldiers' letters had to be censored by an officer, perhaps prudent but certainly a distasteful job. One learnt to skim them quickly for forbidden place names or dates and forget anything else one's eye had picked up. One of the worst crimes in my book was for an officer to joke, in however well-meaning a way, about something in a letter he had censored; it only happened once.

An officer had to certify on his honour that there was nothing censorable in his own letters, which was cramping. One could describe events, guardedly, some weeks after they had taken place, but nobody wanted to write home and worry their family with tales of action. The weather and the countryside thus made up a good deal of one's subject matter. I hated fountain pens and always wrote with a Relief nib and a bottle of ink, which had to stay behind with my books in my bedroll when we were in the line. I noticed when re-reading my letters to Louise that the pen and ink ones are fairly relaxed and, within official limits, informative; while all those scribbled in pencil stick rather grimly to the scenery and to fervent wishes that I were with her.

Finn had wrenched a knee badly at Cassino but made little of it. I now saw it for the first time, grotesquely swollen after all his driving, and packed him off, protesting, to hospital. I learned how much I depended on him, and how much time he saved me by common sense and forethought.

I found the ragged shreds of Italian I had picked up in Eritrea very useful, and tried to add to them by talking to everyone I came across in Castelfrentano. Since I knew nothing of the grammar, I had to make do in all cases with the infinitive of the verb, and take various other short cuts, which seemed to work excellently with the peasantry but less well with the more polished. Amongst the latter, good manners led to a visible struggle for control, almost always ending in giggles (f) or loud laughter (m).

Our new colonel arrived, Gordon reverting to Second-in-Command, which struck me as unjust and which I illogically converted into a prejudice against the C.O. 'Moggs' Hill had been transferred from the Camerons to the Seaforths, and had been Second-in-Command of a battalion in Burma. He was an agile, quick-moving little man, as fast in his thinking as in his movements, with a peculiarly alert, enquiring expression, rather bird-like since he often cocked his head to one side when he was listening to one. It must have been difficult for him to take over at that time, though he gave no impression of it; indeed I never saw him ruffled by anything. We put on a show for him and for the townsfolk by parading the pipes and drums, which was such a success that the following evening George Robertson of D Company, a truly excellent piper, played in the square to a full house.

As usual when we were not in the line, the mobile bath unit was an immediate requirement, as was very often the less mobile dis-infestation unit. Here we had the use of the bath for a couple of hours one morning, and the company, like a vast rugger team after the match, marched by platoons into the temporarily-converted barn. In the dinner hour, after C was clean and before D Company arrived for their turn, I nipped down myself. While I luxuriated in the hot shower and snowdrifts of carbolic lather, the door opened and in came the C.O. and Adjutant and RSM; through the steam I could see that they were escorting someone gleaming with red tabs and rows of medal ribbons, clearly a very superior general. At Sandhurst we had been taught military comportment in various unlikely circumstances, such as how to salute while steering a bicycle with one hand and carrying a map case in the other; but a bath-house rencontre, with one party clad only in a piece of soap, had not been one of them. There was nothing for it but to spring smartly to attention. Unfortunately I chose the end of a half-submerged duckboard which reared up, threw me off and then crashed down into several inches of dirty, soapy water.

When I got back, Owens told me that all company commanders had to report in ten minutes to battalion HQ to meet the Corps Commander. I just got there in time to line up with the others. Lt. General Allfrey, his uniform still drenched, spoke to each of us, but paused when he came to me. 'Haven't I met you before some-where?' I was about to deny vigorously any previous acquaintance when I realized that the question wasn't quite as deadpan as it sounded.

Moggs was still only getting the feel of the battalion when we were suddenly sent up into the line to take over from the 1st/9th Gurkhas. I set off with a recce party on April 16th, waited at Poggio Fiorito until dusk and then walked in the safety of darkness to our destination, Arielli, which C Company was to garrison until, it turned out, May 6th. I spent the next day getting a run-down on our and the enemy positions, went back that night to battalion HQ to explain the set-up, and returned before dawn to Arielli. It was, or had been, a small town, large enough at least to have three churches, as badly smashed up as every other building. It stood on a peninsula of high ground jutting into a broad, shallow valley; the route to it along the neck of the peninsula was covered by machine guns from across the valley and impassable in daylight. There were no inhabitants apart from the Gurkhas, myriads of rats and, at night, the Germans who saucily patrolled the streets at one end of the town.

April 18th was eventful. The place was given a drub-bing in the afternoon from mortars; as soon as it was dark I sent back guides to bring up the company, again in Mac's charge. The Gurkhas had been in Arielli too long and were glad to get out, which was fortunately achieved without any more bombing or shelling to disturb the take-over. Water could only be drawn at night since the well was in full view of the enemy, so a first task was to send out a fighting patrol-cum-water party, under the CSM since the officers were up to the neck in organizing the platoon positions. There were a few shots, and the party came back with twelve prisoners, one of the Jocks wounded in the scuffle. I asked battalion HQ for an escort, and sent out a couple of men to guide it; they promptly picked up another two of the enemy. Another party brought back some water, and we settled down to our first night of watchfulness.

Our elation was damped when the Germans turned out to be Ukrainians and were more properly if less excitingly to be termed deserters than prisoners. They had apparently been forcibly enlisted in 1941 and had at last seen an opportunity to break away from their NCO-warders. Their arrival caused an immense thrill to the psychological warriors at Army HQ who produced plans to set up a vastly magnified loudspeaker system in Arielli to bellow encouragement in Russian to other likely deserters. This I vetoed, and Moggs backed me up. Poor souls, they could never find a place near enough the enemy to be effective where the troops in the line would tolerate their apparatus.

I had a fourth platoon under command from B Company, because the Arielli position was an extensive one. Three platoons manned houses on the edges of the town overlooking the valley and the German positions, while a fourth had the job of going out as a standing patrol to occupy a solitary house in a risky area. We sent out at least one fighting patrol every night, as did the Germans, though we quickly put a stop to their getting into the town; and we always had a wiring or mining party out. In daytime both sides lay up, shooting through loopholes at anything that moved. The little garrison was completed by a gunner O.P. which could call down pre-arranged defensive fire from the divisional artillery, a couple of miles behind us, and in daylight carried out shoots on likely targets.

The enemy, perhaps piqued by the desertions, gave us a bad time the following day with some heavy stonks which got fiercer after dark. The mule train coming up with rations caught it badly, and the top storey of company HQ's house was blown off, while 13 Platoon had to beat off a resolute attack and suffered some casualties in the process. This, the usual pattern, meant that sleep was taken in catnaps during the day by those off duty. We slept soft when we could sleep, for the cellars of our various buildings were piled with old mattresses, alive with fleas which looked on C Company as manna. I found it possible to get by with four hours sleep in the twenty-four, taken in snatches and itches.

I hated the idea of the nightly standing patrol in what was nicknamed Harrington House. It seemed pointless, and I learned that it had been done every night for three months. Regular repetition of a routine can be suicidal, and with Mogg's approval I called it off. We left it well mined and ignored it for forty-eight hours, when we hoped it would be re-occupied, and then put down a shoot which destroyed it totally. The brigadier arrived just before first light one morning and spent the day with us, though there was little he could be shown without being sniped at; I was relieved that he approved my abandoning the standing patrol. He was followed a few days later by Moggs, who made the round of the platoons and then sat out in the sun for a while in the only corner of the ruined square not under enemy observation. Fortunately the stench and the over-fed flies drove him indoors just before a salvo of mortar bombs came down. I think this was the day when shelling set fire to several houses which we needed to keep intact as part of our perimeter. We finally doused the flames with the entire water ration for the day; curiously we were not shot up although most of the fire-fighting was in full view of the enemy.

The flies were increasingly troublesome as the weather grew warmer. The town of course was piled with every sort of filth and rubbish, and inevitably we had some dysentery cases in addition to losses from mortar bombs and machine-gun fire. But the company was in good nick. It was on its own, always popular, and it had a clearly defined role, which it knew it was doing competently. The Jocks were not rattled by the rather eerie life in

Arielli, and patrolled cheerfully and with skill. That was a good test of morale, because setting off in the dark, as a member of a small party—from three or four up to fifteen, depending on whether the function was reconnaisance or fighting—is a cold-blooded venture into any sort of trouble, from an enemy patrol to a new minebelt. Much depends on confidence in the patrol leader, and C Company was well off for good platoon commanders. The men were out on patrol perhaps once in nine or ten nights, but the officers were out every other night with the exception of their company commander, sweating with anxiety until they were back. It was sometimes very silent at night as I sat by the HQ phone, only an occasional bang as a cat set off a trip-wired mine; it was then that the patrolling seemed more dangerous, and I worried more, than on the nights when the Germans were nervous and shot off everything they had.

Robin Collier rejoined and took over his old platoon after convalescing from his Cassino wound, and Mac, who had been doing wonders, was shifted by Moggs to what I hoped would be an easier job. Bobby Burns came to C Company as second-in-command; he had been in charge of the Pioneer platoon and was skilled in laying and defusing any sort of explosive charge. Like anybody with that kind of expertise, he was cool and almost dismayingly brave in any situation. He settled in very quickly, for of course we all knew him and liked him, and I found it a marked relief from pressure to have a second-in-command again for the first time since Ian's death.

Finn, too, rejoined from hospital in excellent form and I resumed the luxury of shaving in hot water. It was like old times to see my spare socks, newly washed by him, neatly draped over a signal wire to dry in the sun. My obsession with feet had worked its way through the whole company. Whenever we marched off into action, every man carried a spare pair of socks, as essential a part of his fighting equipment as his weapon. There was usually no chance of washing them, but it kept one going to change sweaty stinking socks for a pair which, if still dirty, had at least aired out a little. Foot hygiene reached its apogee when I found the off-duty men in one of the platoons washing their feet in tubs of vinegar-smelling wine, the *vendange* in reverse. Wine of some description was to be found in every abandoned village and farmhouse, but only once did I have an instance of men getting drunk, in an outlying section. They were very far from being incapable but I put the fear of God into them by telling them that they could be shot for drunkenness in the face of the enemy, and ordered Owens to stave in every cask in that particular house. The smell and discomfort of a cellar full of sour wine was unbelievable, and to have to remain there was sufficient punishment for the men, though not of course for their section commander.

Our gunner guests changed every few days. Each new F.O.O. made us aware of how badly we and Arielli stank, but a couple of days brought him down to our noisome level. One was a skilled draughtsman who employed his talents in embellishing a careful plan I made of our and the German positions for the benefit of our successors. The result was entrancing, and it was with deep regret that I handed it over in due course. He was far better company than another F.O.O. who had heard such tales of life in Arielli that he refused, day and night, to be parted from his loaded revolver, always at the ready. He even ate one-handed, as though he were in a Wild West film.

May 1st brought the official opening of the malaria season, and the 6th our relief by a Punjabi battalion. The handover was accomplished quietly, though we had to take our final casualty back with us, Pte. Turner of 13 Platoon who was hit by a mortar bomb splinter. The battalion went back into brigade reserve where we could wash and rest despite sporadic shelling, and abandon our grimy battledress for the comfort of drill shirts and shorts.

Arielli had done the company good. Our casualties had not been too heavy, the standard of performance high and the quality of individual officers and men shown in a way that the muddle of Cassino had made impossible. We naturally had not the depth of experience that had been available in the old C Company, where in any section there were two or three men fully capable of leading it when necessary, but we were at last an effective fighting unit, and a cheerful one.

There was a ditty called *Dougal*, with a catchy tune, popular in the old battalion at sing-songs and smokers. Amongst other adventures in many verses, Dougal finds himself on a royal parade, and of course such a fine figure of a recruit catches the monarch's eye:

> *. . . so the King says tae me*
> *'Oh Dougal mon, hoo do ye do?*
> *Oh Dougal mon, hoo do ye do?*
> *Ach, I like yer way an' I like yer style—*
> *Come up tae the paalace an' stay for a while . . .'*

Doing things with a way and in style was almost second nature for the old regulars. It was something the young volunteers and conscripts of wartime learned for themselves. They would sing zestfully

> *I don't want to be a soldier.*
> *I don't want to go to war. . .*

but since they were soldiers and had been sent to war, they were encouraged by the regiment to feel that they might as well carry it off with an air. Doing things in style was an important aspect of morale.

No unit can keep going unless it is well administered. The forward troops must be able to take for granted that in almost any conditions their essential needs will be met, that ammunition and grub will somehow arrive. We did not expect the impossible in the way of replacement boots or clothing when we were in the line, though some kit could be taken from the dead if they had not been killed too messily; so after a week or two we were a scruffy bunch. Curiously, everyone shaved whenever there was an opportunity, despite an endemic shortage of razor blades, for the sake of comfort rather than smartness.

Back in rest, we could count on the battalion's B Echelon meeting us with our baggage—basically the men's packs or kitbags containing their clean shirts and socks and underwear—and on the Quartermaster's having dug out of division the kit we needed to replace ripped uniforms or disintegrating boots. No need to issue orders to get the dirt off and smarten up, it was every soldier's first aim. It felt glorious to be in a clean shirt, though less so when it had come back from being baked to kill the lice.

It was with a light heart that I handed over to Bobby on the news that I had come up on the leave roster, with Bill Garroch and forty of the men. Bill evidently would take no chances with an official leave camp, for his luggage consisted of a sandbag full of bottles to celebrate my impending birthday. In fact, there was very little drinking in the battalion, even when drink was to be had; my mess bill for two and a half months, carefully delivered to me in Arielli, read 'Two bottles whisky 17/-'.

It was a 250-mile journey past olive trees knee-deep in young oats and barley to the rest camp at Bari, where the dormitory seemed a little chilly after the flea-infested fug of the Arielli cellars. I met a number of old friends from other units in the division, celebrated my twenty-fifth birthday, went to a couple of concerts in the city, at last found an opportunity of going to Communion, and after four days went back.

That was a day. I left Bari in the morning with the leave party in a three-tonner, travelling by way of Foggia and Termoli, and at 8.30 in the evening found our B Echelon. I was wanted forward at once, and reached battalion HQ a couple of hours later, to learn that the previous night C Company had counter-attacked and recaptured a position where the Germans had over-run the Frontier Force Rifles. I pushed on up to the F.F.R. HQ under whose command the company had come, and finally about midnight arrived at C, to congratulate them all. There had been only a few losses in the assault thanks to the skill of Bobby's plan and the dashing verve with which it had been carried out.

The German infantry did not attack again but the position was heavily mortared in the small hours. Three men were killed and Andy was very badly smashed up; he died two hours later. It was not a healthy place, and as soon as it was light I moved company HQ and set all the platoons to digging in; only after completing slit trenches for the living did we turn to graves for the dead. Andy's death was a heavy loss. He had been unfailingly cheerful even in the worst patches and he had the great knack of lifting his men's spirits in tune with his own. He exemplified, as had Ian, Maréchal Lyautey's dictum that an essential ingredient in the make-up of the good officer is gaiety. I can't think of anything worse than serving with someone like the Miller of Dee who 'laughed and sang from morn till night'; but of two men equipped in all other ways, the one with the merry heart will always be the better leader.

The following day was a quiet one without casualties. We spent that night re-rigging and thickening-up the wire and putting mines down, and twenty-four hours later were relieved by D Company, but not before another three men were killed in the early evening. All told, we lost one officer and nine men killed in this affair, with rather more than a dozen wounded. I felt proud of the company. I noted when we got out of the line in what good heart the Jocks were, despite the death of friends; I wasn't very cheerful myself, immersed in the dismal business of writing letters to the relatives. We had not reached the stage of envying some one with a slight wound, enough to ensure a few weeks between sheets in a hospital bed: that came later. The dead were talked about and they were clearly missed, particularly in their own platoon and section, perhaps even unobtrusively mourned by close friends. But that was all; life, and the campaign, went on, the rain had stopped and it was sunny again, we were no longer in that unpleasant position, and Corporal Ball was once again feeding us in his incomparable way. This was not stark insensitivity, I believed, but a realization that it would be impossible to go on if you thought too much about burying the friend with whom you'd shared a mess tin for months. It could lead to wondering who would bury you.

Unlike any other management situation, command in war means the inescapable condemnation of some individuals to wounds or death in the process of achieving the object. This unpalatable fact is masked for the fireside strategist by images of omelettes and eggs, and for the higher command is transformed, as it must be, into a mathematical equation. An 'acceptable' level of casualties in a given operation may be 25 per cent, the acceptability depending on the importance of the objective, the support that can be called on and the availability of fresh troops. Conversely, if a particular unit or formation has been hard-pressed for a long time or has already suffered heavy losses, it might be thought capable of sustaining only 10 or 15 per cent casualties before ceasing to be effective. Clearly, the better the unit, the longer it can go on, although it is usually believed that one third casualties in a single operation will put a unit out of action, at least for the time being. The commander will do everything in his power to minimize the casualty rate by the way he plans and fights his battle, but casualties there will be.

For the battalion, in most cases, the equations have been calculated higher up, and it is committed. At the company and platoon level, maths get left behind, the percentages have faces and characters, attached to people one knows very well after living and working together for months or years. Every order for an attack, for instance, carries the unspoken message 'This means that you, or you, or I, will probably be dead in the morning'. What prevents this becoming intolerable is the Russian roulette implicit in 'or'; the platoon or company commander doesn't know who it is going to be, and he and his men are alike sanguine that it will be somebody else who gets the chop. The fact that your optimism has been justified if you do come out unhurt is another of the reasons for the philosophic attitude men take to the death of friends.

It was not difficult to decide whether or not the company was in good form. To know how the individual soldier was bearing up formed one of the most important parts of the platoon commander's job, which he could only do well with good corporals in charge of his three sections. The platoon is the private soldier's family, and it is within the family that stresses show up and must be remedied. It is in barrack-room life that soldiers can sometimes get across one another, which may require judicious posting between platoons; the conditions and dangers of active service inevitably generate tension, but seldom in my experience between individuals. The corporal has to be the lightning conductor for his section, absorbing the worries and strains of the soldiers and so enabling them to stick it out. And this is trebly true of the platoon commander. By virtue of his commissioned rank, he is not only the first to stand up when the shooting starts, it is he who carries the collective burden of strain for his twenty or twenty-five men.

We still had one platoon forward, which I relieved every other day. For the other platoons it was relatively peaceful, and very comfortable; a bivvy erected over a rectangle dug down three feet made a roomy little tent with all the comforting safety of a slit trench. Home mail arrived again, which included letters from Ian Jack's widow and the mother of a lance-corporal killed at Cassino. I prosed away once more to the company officers about the importance of writing at once, honestly and not sanctimoniously, to the next of kin. The first step in doing so was to get that deadening piece of officialese out of one's head, and think instead of a man's wife or his mother: but why, I wonder now, never his father? My only contribution to the war at this stage was to take out a patrol one night when I wasn't changing the platoons around. It consisted of Robin and six Jocks whom I picked carefully, and unnecessarily since nothing whatever happened. We got back in the small hours, drenched from crawling through dew-soaked corn, when Robin was so unwise as to say he had a bottle of whisky in his bivvy. One circuit from hand to mouth round the eight of us was the end of that bottle.

To my intense regret David Douglas left the battalion about this time for a job at Corps HQ. I had not seen much of him since we had arrived in Italy but it had always been good to know that he was around somewhere with his company. There were very few links left now with the original 2nd Battalion, although we narrowly missed one in the shape of Andy, our old C.O. He escaped from the P.O.W. camp where he had been imprisoned since Tobruk, and in deplorable rags, with a borrowed flock of goats, successfully passed through the German lines. By a marvellous coincidence he walked into the 4th Indian Division (and was fairly crusty with an officer who didn't immediately recognize in this tatterdemalion goatherd Brigadier Anderson D.S.O., M.C., late of 11th Brigade); if only it had been the Camerons who received him!

By now, the end of May, the countryside was superbly lovely, although it required a conscious effort to look at it as landscape and not as an actual or potential battlefield. The nightingales sang even through a mortar bombardment and the fire-flies were out in glittering squadrons. It was odd to see no animals at all, not even a rabbit. But this tranquil enjoyment ran counter to one of Mogg's cardinal principles, 'prevention of stagnation', which I sometimes thought ruefully meant impatience with any one sitting still for half an hour, rather as grown-ups harass children: 'If you've nothing better to do than read a book, you'd better go and help Aunt So-and-So.' Moggs Hill was such a vivid and lively C.O. that stagnation under his command was about as likely as a strip-tease at a Wee Free social, but he was delighted when we got on the move again with the division.

*　*　*

C Company found itself on the right flank of the allied army in Italy, an honour that meant less than the fact that we were on the shore, with only a vineyard and a low cliff between us and the sea. I took over some filthy houses but kept the company out in the open in bivvies and ordered twice daily bathing parades, knowing that this was too good to last. It was delightful to find that the army could spare thought from the task of beating the Germans for the care of civilian susceptibilities; we were strictly ordered, to Moggs's hooting derision, to let no man bathe naked. It was exhilarating to hear that the enemy had fallen back in the western sector and abandoned Rome. Three days later came the long-awaited landings in France; it seemed a long time since all those demands in America for an instant Second Front. We talked quite seriously of one more big shove clearing the Germans out of Italy, and of the war in Europe being over by Christmas. On a more local level, we had Robin's twenty-first birthday to celebrate.

I am hazy on how we got news about the progress of the war or about what was happening at home. The army ran a newspaper, and I think there was a radio at B Echelon which picked up the Forces Broadcasts and news summaries, from which battalion HQ issued a news sheet. We certainly never felt cut off from news of what was happening. The picture of the current battle was an integral part of orders; 'information about own troops' always followed 'information about enemy'. When there was no occasion for issuing fresh orders, information was always passed on down the company as in much detail as we received it — most important, because factual news, good or bad, is better for morale than rumour. Hence the let-down at Cassino where the battalion could get hold of scarcely any news which we could pass on to the men.

We set off up the Adriatic coast in great style. The Germans were withdrawing but in fits and starts, fighting desperately to retain this or that position before suddenly abandoning it, and imposing enough delay on the advance to permit the full fortification of the Gothic Line, further north in the Apennines. This was planned as the last redoubt, another Cassino, but we were made to fight nearly all the way to get to it through a terrain of steep east–west ridges, ideal for defence. Our first mark was the seaside town of Pescara, the approaches to which were heavily mined. Someone at division had the brainwave of using DUKWs, amphibious vehicles, to outflank the minefields and get into the town itself. Since the occupation of Pescara had been allotted by Moggs to C Company, I could enliven the usual drill of issuing my orders to the platoon commanders by detailing one of them to advance by boat. Robin embarked his platoon, with some of the battalion's pioneers to lift mines, and sailed away while the rest of the company enviously plodded up the main road when, we hoped, the more salient mines had been cleared. No shooting ahead, which was encouraging, and when we eventually reached the place we found Robin and his twenty men lording it in a totally empty town; no inhabitants, no Germans. The town is bisected by the River Pescara, the only bridge having been somewhat inefficiently blown, for a single steel girder remained.

The DUKWs had long since returned, and we had to get across somehow. Bobby Burns was a great lad for finding a way, and turned up with the news that a patrol had found intact a racing eight, evidently the property of the Pescara Rowing Club; he had already worked out in his head how many trips would be required to ferry the company across, assuming Bow and No. 2 would have to row it back each time. It was a beguiling prospect, the more so since I hadn't handled an oar since Eights Week in 1939, but I quailed at the prospect of drowning a wholly dry-bob company in instalments and insisted on the girder, with Bobby and a few trusties in the eight as a longstop. Nobody fell off the girder, six inches wide, but it was a horrid business to cross it.

Once over, we pushed on fast, anxious to get out of the town which had been thoroughly and ingeniously booby-trapped, and glad to have had no casualties. I was always thoroughly frightened of booby-traps. Mines are usually laid where men or vehicles are likely to pass, and sometimes one could guess from a disturbance in the soil that their presence was at least a strong possibility. In the days before mine-detectors, the battalion pioneers, or the Sappers if we were lucky, would probe for them with thin wires, lying on their bellies as they did so. Having located the buried mine, they would 'disarm' it, which sounds simple but required technical knowledge of the particular type of mine, steady hands and icy courage. Mine detectors are actuated by the presence of metal. To defeat them the Germans evolved the *schu* mine, made of wood; to step on one meant losing a foot and, usually, an eye. Booby traps were even worse, consisting of a mine or other explosive charge usually fired by a trip wire. This could be fixed to a door handle or a lavatory plug or any other object liable to be pulled or pushed. Other booby traps were operated by release of pressure, so that they would go off when you picked something up. On the whole, setting them up probably absorbed more time than was justified by the resulting casualties, but they could be highly unnerving to advancing troops.

Still no Germans in the farms and villages, but an ecstatic welcome with flowers and embraces from the people. This was war at its best, a long succession of civic receptions jumbled up with garden fêtes: it is only the complete absence of an enemy that makes a soldier feel heroic. Too good to last, grumped the old sweats through their festoons of roses, and of course they were right, but it ended not in a bloody encounter with the enemy but a lightning transfer to the Mountain Warfare School at Campobasso. The implications were obvious, and I didn't relish them, but kept my feelings to myself. Every unit has one or two licensed croakers, men who unfailingly predict rain, or an interruption of mail, or leave can-cellations, or heavy fighting ahead, usually to the hilarity of the others. I came to the conclusion that they were useful because they got out into the open the forebodings any sensible fellow would have, forebodings much less oppressive when given an airing by somebody else. There was one essential pre-condition, that the croaker must himself be a good soldier. If he were a bad one, he would just be a malcontent, and must go. Any NCO or officer who showed any sign of the trait had to go even faster, of course.

We spent nearly a month camped near Campobasso, Moggs and the instructors from the School putting us violently through the hoop. I ran a cadre for the battalion NCOs which began at 6.15 with P.T., for which I sub-stituted the dancing of reels, and continued till dusk with map reading and compass work, followed by night ops after dark. We then ran up and down the hills on com-pany exercises until we could climb 4,000 feet with full kit and ammunition and do some soldiering at the top, and worked up to three-day battalion exercises. It was good to be up amongst the Abruzzi peaks at daybreak after a night of marching and counter-marching, to watch the charcoal-burners tending their slow-smoulder-ing piles, to unload the primuses from the mules and brew up the dawn char. I found my legs stood up to climbing pretty well, but coming down the hills again was hell, on one knee in particular. When there was nobody shooting at us, as here, there was time to notice it.

We had some fun as well as much hard work. Campo-basso had a cinema, well patronized, and I found a superb swimming hole in a big burn near the company's bivvy area where we went by platoons to wash off the sweat in the icy green water. We had a lot of inter-company visiting during our rare periods off duty, since it was a long time since the whole battalion had been within strolling distance. We took it in turns to mount a full battalion guard. I thought I knew that C Company was still capable of a smart turn-out and good drill despite the battering of the last six months, but even I was surprised at the excellence of the guard mounting, one of the army's treasured little ceremonies. To my pleasure, Moggs broke off a conference he was holding in order to watch, and like a good C.O. congratulated Owens, as CSM and hence responsible, as well as the sergeant and men of the guard. The company was pleased, and boasted accordingly: 'Will ye stop bummin' yer chat about yer drill?' I overheard an irritated man from another company ask, with some justification.

On July 4th I took a party of twenty men from the company to Cassino. It was a strange occasion, clear skies and sunshine instead of the interminable sleet and snow, silence in place of the gunfire and bomb explosions, freedom to walk about in full daylight. After prowling around I found the hole where Owens and I had spent three weeks, and measured it; strange that two men, and Owens was a big fellow, could live in a cavity four feet by five, with three feet of headroom under the sand-bag roof. Even stranger to walk the seventy-five yards to the crest of Point 593 and look at the well-sited, carefully constructed dugouts the Germans had lived in, and then go on slightly downhill to what had been the monastery. It consisted of acres and acres of rubble, heaped up to form hillocks and valleys, here and there a stump of marble or fragment of mosaic. The view was stupendous in every direction, and when one lowered one's gaze almost every corner of the valleys leading to Cassino lay open; what an observation post! Standing on the summit of the biggest heap of broken masonry was a make-shift altar of ammunition boxes draped with a tattered cloth, surmounted by a cross of two charred sticks, a legacy of the Poles' fearful victory; over a thousand of them were buried there. It was the only Christian symbol on what had been consecrated ground since the monastery's foundation 1,400 years ago, a suitable point for reflection on the nature of man in St. Benedict's day and in our own. But there was no time for that sort of thing, the war was still waiting and the Jocks and I had to get back to it.

Letters from Louise had been describing what were still called robot planes and their effect on life and work in London—fire-watching from the Embassy roof, the nightly decision over whether or not to go down to the basement from her top-floor flat, sitting for hours in the dark in trains trying to enter or leave London in a raid. My anxiety increased when Moggs learned that his house in London had been blown to pieces, though mercifully his wife was safe. His son had been killed six months earlier, his brother only a few weeks ago. He felt these losses very deeply but only revealed occasionally and accidentally his grief; it was private, and not part of his job in commanding what he had made into a very good battalion.

On July 15th we were off to the central sector where we battled away until October up the central ridge of Italy. It was a vicious little campaign through Tuscany, with no major set piece but with continual fighting at brigade and battalion level as we pushed the enemy off one position after another, and always up and down hill. Like all moves, it began with an advance party on which I took Robin and Finn. It was only when we were on our way that I realized that Finn was ill as a result of something he had eaten. As with everything he did, he was very neat when he was sick over the side of the jeep. The long journey over wildly twisting roads must have been purgatory, but he never uttered a word of complaint.

We did our recce, and were joined by the battalion near Arezzo. Moggs called his O Group together and gave us his usual rather curt, crystal-clear orders; like any good C.O., he distinguished sharply between a company commanders' conference, to hammer out a training programme or the implications of a battalion move, and the issuing of orders. I had C Company in Puglia, a little town just evacuated by the Germans, from which we patrolled energetically. The people showed more hatred of the Germans than we had encountered so far, and also —at least among the peasants—far stronger anti-fascist feelings than in the south. It was in Tuscany that the partisans were a reality and not a post-war myth, and very valuable they proved. They were adamant that the Germans had left behind them fascist sympathizers equipped with radio sets. One had to discount a large element of paying off old scores, but I took one story sufficiently seriously to take some men to the next village and arrest 'a prominent Fascist'. I felt rather like Himmler as we crashed into his house in the middle of the night, but in this case at least, I learned a week later from our Intelligence Officer, David Galloway, the partisans had been quite right.

Our patrols soon located the enemy in a series of sharp skirmishes, taking prisoners, killing Germans and suffering losses. Taking prisoners was essential for intelligence purposes, but we had to fight for them. On the night of the 24th Bill Garroch was out patrolling and bumped a

REZZO: H.M. King George VI with officers of the 4th Indian Division.
The two Camerons are 'Moggs' Hill and Teddy Cameron

Private Finn; Major David Douglas

ORSOGNA: The three platoons of C Company. Robin Collier is sitting amongst his men in the top snapshot

strongpoint; he was put out of action almost at once with
a shin smashed by one bullet and the calf muscle on the
other leg torn away by another. 44 Macdonald was also
wounded. Sgt. Winton took command and carried on,
killing three Germans and bringing one back. It was more
difficult to bring Bill back, for he was built like a steer.
Two Jocks were completely exhausted when they carried
him in, and could never have done it without the help of
Aldo, a partisan who had attached himself to C Company.
Aldo was a light-hearted and very brave young man who
always put on a hairnet when he went out with the
patrols. Death was a risk he faced calmly, but not the
prospect of mussing his elegant locks.

The padre came up and gave us a service at Puglia; it
was a thin congregation consisting of company HQ and
the few men who could safely be brought back from the
reserve platoon. Like almost all ministers of the Church
of Scotland, he was a good preacher, and gave us that
day an excellent sermon on the text 'I will give back to
you the years that the locusts have eaten'. During most
of my service, the battalion was not fortunate in its
padres (I remember one nicknamed The Looter by the
Jocks, and indeed he did seem more interested in objects
than in souls), although I was told that during the desert
fighting in 1941 and 1942 the then padre was a wonderful
man. In Italy too we had a good man in Captain the
Reverend Dick, who never strove to be popular and so
achieved it effortlessly, and never felt the need to display
a spurious manliness as did some chaplains. The effect of a
good padre made one realize how much the battalion had
missed when we had second-rate ones.

Whenever it was possible, as in most of the Tuscan
fighting, I kept the company cookhouse going and had
hot food brought up in containers to the forward positions
rather than send up rations for a platoon brew-up; good
food ranked just below the importance of sound feet in my
creed, and the platoons were amateurs compared to Ball

and his two assistant cooks. He had to use what was sent up to him —fortunately he never found a hedgehog to bake in clay, an experience he promised I would never forget —and his ingenuity made something palatable of almost everything, including the early versions of dehydrated foods which now began to reach us. The potatoes defeated even him; I heard a Jock one day agreeing that most of the processed rations were good 'but I canna stick they hydraulic spuds'. The ration quite often included flour, though very seldom any baking powder. The canteen back at B Echelon had a supply of Andrews Liver Salts one day, most of which Ball snapped up, and triumphantly produced scones and rock cakes for the whole company. They were very good to eat, and doubtless just as good for our innards. The trick caught on, and there was soon almost theological controversy between the company cookhouses on whether one got a lighter pastry with Andrews or Enos.

It was at this time that the division was visited by the King. Moggs and a party of officers and men paraded for his inspection, very appropriately because he was Colonel-in-Chief of the regiment. With a royal eye for faces, he recognized Charlie Cameron (younger brother of Alan who had been with C Company in 1940) as having mounted a Sovereign's Guard at Balmoral. It was also now that the company was in among the medals again, CSM Owens and one of our corporals being awarded the M.M. and Bobby the M.C. for the counter-attack on the over-run Frontier Force position.

On we went, the company's next breathing space being a village which we took by infiltrating round the flank and threatening the Germans' line of withdrawal. Some effective bren-gun fire got them out without the need for a frontal attack. They clearly had not reckoned on leaving so soon, for little damage had been done; usually the Germans smashed everything before laying mines and withdrawing. I found myself with company HQ in a fine house with vaulted ceiling, and still furnished with tables and chairs. We had crept into it at 2 a.m. ready for a fight, and were paralysed for a moment by an eldritch noise which turned out to come from a hen. The poor thing was instantly despatched and later served by Finn, the table properly laid with a white cloth. I noticed again here how careful the men were with abandoned Italian property, even though breaking up someone else's belongings might have been thought a release from strain or a back-handed swipe at the bloody war.

We spent a couple of days here, probing forward with patrols to establish the next line of enemy positions before attacking. We took a small town called Marcena where Moggs came up to see us and plan the next move; we were at a tip of a little salient, and in fact at that point C Company was ahead of all the other allied forces. Aldo had left us because we had advanced out of his countryside and instead we had an Italian captain attached. This was useful since I found myself the temporary mayor of Marcena, organizing food distribution and a medical clinic. I set up my HQ in an even grander situation, a palazzo of great elegance, cypress trees round a very fine sunken garden, fountains with carp and goldfish in the basins and once an hour a salvo of heavy shells plopping into the back courtyard —the German gunners hadn't registered it quite accurately. The owners had fled, perhaps because their sympathies were too well known to the townsfolk, leaving behind an old caretaker and a dog, both promptly put on the ration strength by the Jocks and fed from the cookhouse.

We attacked again, C Company taking Bibbiano, a large village. Although we had a brisk fight for it, the Germans had planned their withdrawal well. The strangest aspect of their preparations lay on the table of what had evidently been their HQ, a copy in English of *Lord Jim*. I poked at it gingerly with a long pole, fearing it was booby-trapped. When nothing exploded I picked it

151

up, to find an inscription, also in English, on the fly leaf: 'Good luck, old fellow, and pray to Him that you'll return unwounded to your Merry Old England that has been and will never come again. We are convinced to win the war. Look at my leaflet. What do you think now? — A German Soldier.' The leaflet, with a crude drawing, declared that we were fighting and dying far away from home where 'the Yanks have lots of money and lots of time to chase after your women'. It was sheer bad luck for A German Soldier, whom I respected as a Conrad lover, that his missive had reached about the only man in the division with a Yank wife.

Bibbiano lay just beneath the crest of a long 2,000 foot ridge, the battalion objective. A Company captured Monte Grillo on the ridge but were immediately counter-attacked in great strength. A tremendous fight ensued, two platoons being over-run in their positions and the battle continuing room by room in the HQ building, with a final desperate assault by the third platoon in an attempt to restore the situation. Some men escaped to make their way back, but in effect that was the end of A Company. C was ordered to re-take the position that night, and I took the platoon commanders forward in the afternoon to look at the ground. The trouble was that there was too much of it, a big expanse of rough grass and rock with two commanding hillocks on the crest of the ridge; and by now C, like the other companies, was much below strength. There was a full moon that night which hindered as much as it helped us. We got up to our jump-off line, down came our artillery and down came their defensive fire, and we belted up the hillside, two platoons forward. Robin's platoon reached the left-hand hillock in their first rush, cutting through the defence with seven enemy dead and a prisoner, but on the right the other leading platoon was heavily embroiled with what turned out to be the Germans' main position. I committed the third platoon but the defence still far outnumbered us, so I took a deep breath and decided to pull the company out. I was thankful to get Robin's men back without too many more casualties; he was as canny in the ticklish business of withdrawing as he had been dashing in the attack. For his leadership in the action he was later awarded the M.C. The battalion took a bloody nose in the attack on this five mile long ridge; the whole brigade was committed the next day, but it took another four days to capture it.

Meanwhile we were back in Bibbiano, licking our wounds and not relishing an unaccustomed sense of failure, which had made the company angry rather than depressed. The village was regularly and heavily shelled but the houses were strongly built and we did not come to much harm. I wrote to Louise one night describing the command post; a signaller awake by his set but everybody else grunting under his blanket, the flame in the hurricane lamp jumping up and down as the 210 mm shells exploded, and the rich pleasure I had in reading in a *New Yorker* she had sent me an advertisement for Chanel's 'Danger'. I wondered whether Mme Chanel had ever really savoured the smell that men give off when they are afraid.

On August 9th Moggs Hill came up with his tactical HQ, which really meant his gunner officer and a major from the Central India Horse. He always took pains to keep his battalion in the picture, and apart from planning the next move he wanted to tell me, to pass on to the men, what had been pieced together of A Company's story, and how well they had fought. And he wanted to congratulate us, and in particular Robin and his platoon, on the abortive counter-attack. He was sitting with me in the command post when the shelling began again. The bursts usually came in fours; I heard two, and then everything erupted in an eye-searing flash, though I was conscious of no noise. The room was full of smoke and dust from the broken walls. The first person I could see was Cameron, my signaller, already grey in death, and then beyond him Moggs lying on his back with his eyes open. I knelt beside him. 'I'm finished, Peter,' he said in a quiet, reflective voice; there was a terrible wound in his chest, and his head was hurt too. Our ambulance jeep, fitted with crossbars to carry a pair of stretchers, was undamaged amidst the rubble in the street, and we got Moggs and the gunner, also hit, away at once. Moggs was still alive at the Regimental Aid Post where the M.O. gave him a blood transfusion, but he died an hour or two later. Ironically, we were pulled out of the line the following day and went into rest.

The major from the C.I.H. had left us just before that fatal salvo landed; years later, speaking of the incident, he told me, 'Of course, you had a charmed life.' Remembering Moggs, that rings in my ear almost as an accusation. 'There are no words,' I wrote to Louise at the time, 'to tell you what a sense of loss we feel— the whole battalion collectively as well as a great many of us individually who had come to know him well. He worked incessantly for the benefit of his men, nothing was too much trouble for him, and in action he led us and inspired us as will never happen to us again. I broke down when he died, he had been so good a friend through everything that has happened to his battalion.

'As we had just come out of the line, we were able to bury him as we wanted, with full honours. The ceremony was deeply moving—the band playing a slow march, drums muffled and draped in black, the battalion in full dress marching on in slow time: then the coffin carried on by the pall bearers (I was one), with the flag on it and on top his balmoral, a jagged hole in one side, and laid over the grave, in between the graves of two of our privates who had been killed a few days earlier: the service very well conducted by the chaplain, and then, after the lowering of the coffin, the pipe-major played The Flowers of the Forest which is the lament always used and which tears your heart out: the firing party fire three volleys over the grave: the bugler sounds Last Post and Reveille, and the ceremony is over except that each of his men stepped up to the grave and saluted him for the last time.'

To have served under Andy and Moggs, two commanding officers wholly dissimilar but each men of exceptional distinction, was rare fortune, I knew, which made the latter's death more desolating. After the war Mary Hill, his widow, gave me a pair of his cuff-links which I have worn almost every day since; and every time I have buttoned them into my shirt-sleeves I have thought of Moggs.

* * *

Jamie Thomson, who by now was our Second-in-Command, took over the battalion, and I was stepped up to his old position until a new C.O. should arrive. It was a year and five days since I had taken over C Company, and I felt quite lost without them, although I had the great pleasure of handing them over to Colin Kerr whom I had last seen at Keren. Our rest area was beside Lake Trasimeno, muddy and tepid but still providing an opportunity for everyone to swim. I moved my traps to battalion HQ and found myself in the unusual luxury of a large tent which I shared with Teddy Cameron, our signals officer, and Angus MacKintosh. My job at that point consisted primarily of organising leave parties to Rome and providing some sort of recreation for the remainder of the battalion.

We had been far below strength even before A Company copped it, and now we were down to almost half the battalion's establishment. Jamie Thomson told me to scour the rear areas for any Cameron Highlanders I could find and appeal to Army HQ for reinforcements, and threw in three days leave on top. I took another officer, Bob MacKenzie, with me as well as a spare driver in addition to Finn, since we had an enormous mileage to cover; at least the journey was in a staff car and not a jeep.

We did the usual round of base hospitals to see our wounded and learn to whom they would like a letter sent, and found a few men due to complete their convalescence and therefore about to rejoin. Then on to Caserta, still General Headquarters, where I spent from 11 a.m. to 8 p.m. asking about reinforcements. Robin's father, General Collier, was very helpful in smoothing the path, and thanks to him I saw generals, brigadiers and colonels in eight different offices. At least the point was made that a good battalion needed more men if it were to remain a good battalion, but there were no promises of an instant draft, understandably since Italy was now a sideshow. One of the worst decisions of the war had been implemented immediately after Alexander's final victory at Cassino, when he was robbed of troops for an irrelevant invasion of the south of France; and of course all drafts from the U.K. were now wanted for the main second front campaign.

I felt we had worked for our three days in Rome and was rather nettled to find that the flat which the battalion had taken for leave parties was quite naturally full up. I rebelled at the thought of a leave-camp dormitory five miles outside the city, so walked round the corner and knocked on the door of the first flat I came to, asking if we could be put up for a few days. Signora Avolio was recently widowed, her husband having been shot by the Germans in a totally senseless and random massacre of professional men just before they evacuated Rome. She and her mother-in-law could not have been more kind and welcoming, and it was with the utmost difficulty that I could get them to accept our rations; payment for our accommodation was out of the question despite the evident difficulty of her situation, so proudly concealed. Her son was a young medical student (now a successful doctor in Rome with a charming wife and family of his own); and she and he planned how best we could use our few days. The Avolios were musical, and Bob and I could make some small return of their kindness by taking them

156

to a concert for which we found some black market tickets. Thanks to our hosts, it was a civilized and civilizing interlude.

Back at the battalion we learned that the brigade was about to move up in what was planned as the break-through of the Gothic Line. Our sector was north of Urbino, roughly the eastern side of Italy's spine, and like every other sector was a jumble of hills and ridges with few and dreadful roads. The operation began pleasantly enough with fairly easy marches or lorry trips and nightly camps. The last lap had to be covered on foot with a couple of hundred mules to hump the ammunition and heavy weapons. I was left behind with B Echelon and the job of getting supplies up to the battalion. The divisional ration, ammunition and petrol points shifted daily as the division advanced, and one had to find them before drawing supplies and ferrying them forward. One day it took nine hours for our transport to cover sixteen miles, and on another I noted that the day's rations could not be issued to the companies until 4 a.m. and that the Ration Corporal was off again at 9 to draw the next day's. The three-tonners rolled and swayed on the steep bends much as Hannibal's elephants must have done; if one went over the edge it meant the loss of a company's essential require-ments as well as the lorry and an unfortunate driver. The battalion's needs were not limited to food and ammunition; I had to indent for 500 pairs of boots, at the same time as arguing with division over our bread ration and over alleged kit deficiencies. The Q side tenaciously clung to the belief that one could end a series of actions with as much usable gear as one had started with.

By September 3rd the battalion had reached Monte della Croce, an artificial wilderness cleared of anything that afforded cover. We were lucky to surprise the position by speed and not have to fight for it. Jamie Thomson went forward with the brigadier to recce our next objective, Tavoleto and the San Lorenzo ridge, while I brought the battalion up to the concentration area. We were smartly shelled here, one of the dead being the RSM, Jock Campbell, or Greetin' Jamie as he was known to the men. That night the attack went in, the Camerons assaulting the ridge while the 2nd/7th Gurkhas went for the town. C Company led the way followed by Jamie Thomson and tactical HQ; I had to stay at the main battalion HQ fretting about the company. All went well, and the advance continued over the River Ventano, D having to fight their way over, C unopposed. Next morning, moving forward, the company was stopped by heavy fire, with two men killed and Colin Kerr and others wounded.

Our new C.O. arrived at this juncture, Alistair Noble who had been on the staff of the 10th Indian Division, and whom I had met in 1940 at the depot in Inverness. We were a family-linked regiment; Alistair was younger brother to Tony, adjutant of the old 2nd in the desert. Jamie reverted to Second-in-Command, and I was about to go back to the company when I was despatched to brigade HQ as acting brigade-major while the regular incumbent was having an abscessed tooth dealt with. A B.M. is a lowly form of operations, or G, staff officer, and I found the work of translating the brigadier's plan into detailed orders for the brigade most interesting. The brig — by now Brigadier H. F. C. Partridge, D.S.O. — was patient, which helped, and extremely lucid in his thinking and planning which helped even more. Although I saw a lot of the three battalion HQs, I felt uncomfortably remote from our own people. They did not forget me, however, and sent back a despatch rider with an important-looking letter to me from the War Office. It contained three little bronze oak leaves with instructions to be careful of them and on no account wear one on my greatcoat. The oak leaf is the outward and visible sign that one has been mentioned in a despatch. Since it was more than three years earlier that my name had been mentioned in the despatch recounting the Keren battle, I felt the rider's petrol had been wasted on a wholly non-urgent communication.

The 'independent' Republic of San Marino lay in our path. The tiny state consists almost entirely of a precipitous mountain crowned with the fairy-tale battlements of the city walls. A modern town lay on the lower slopes, and a few villages stood in the well-tilled land round the mountain. Its borders were marked by large crosses cut into the turf and whitened with chalk or lime, to warn off the allied bombers; they hadn't kept out the Germans. For political reasons it was decided that the Camerons rather than our Indian units must take San Marino, though in fact the Italians, after enduring Germans and Americans, Britons, New Zealanders, Poles, French and French Moroccans, gave the highest marks for conduct and behaviour to gl' Indiane. On the other hand, the propaganda broadcasts wouldn't be made by the Italians but by Goebbels.

The brigade orders for the operation were fairly complex because we had some tanks allotted to us as well as the divisional and some corps artillery. I got the orders out and after his usual careful check the brigadier signed them. (Anybody really anxious to outlaw modern war should concentrate on the duplicating machine, not nuclear missiles.) Off went the orders to all concerned and off I went to the battalion to command C Company in the attack, with a lively and personal hope that I had got the timings right for the barrage, the attack and the counterattack supporting fire. It was a salutary experience, to be recommended for all staff officers, and a good example of the transmission of orders down to the actual executant, the private soldier.

As the brigadier's G staff officer, I had to go with him to the divisional commander's Order Group; one sat in the background making notes like fury and busily scribbling with a chinagraph pencil on the talc cover of a map-case. Afterwards there usually followed a few minutes with the G1 —the general's senior staff officer —confirm-ing or clarifying odd points of detail. Then back to brigade, the brigadier signalling en route to his battalion comman-ders and those of the supporting arms allotted to him, and his Q staff, where to meet him; like any commander, down to that of a platoon, he preferred to see the ground with his subordinates before finalizing his plan. If in outline it was already clear in his mind, I would be despatched to start drafting the detailed order from what he told me as we bumped along in his jeep.

Down a step, the process, very familiar to me, was repeated by the C.O., when he had made *his* plan, to the company commanders. At my level, if the company plan was fairly obvious, I could give it to the platoon command-ers only, though if it were complicated or a night operation I liked to pull in sergeants and section commanders. Orders must be positive, no hedging phrases like 'will try to . . .' were permissible: 'C Company will capture and hold so-and-so.' It was important to impart very clearly the mass of information about the method —start line, timings, artillery support, Verey signals, location of HQ, units on our flanks. By this time the broad canvas of the divisional plan had been turned into a very enlarged detail of one corner of the picture.

The platoon commander usually issued his orders to the whole platoon together; most of the information relevant at company level was just as important to the private soldier, so it had to be passed on. The army taught one very well to put across the three cardinal points: the objective; how we were going to achieve it; and the outside support on which we could count in doing so. With this in his head, the soldier could feel that he was going to play his part in a thought-out operation, not just walk into a shambles. Orders were sometimes confirmed in writing below battalion level, as at Arielli when I was sending out fighting patrols. To make sure that our mortars and artillery, as well as the platoons manning the perimeter, were quite clear about a patrol's times and routes in and out, and the signals on which covering fire was to come down, and where, I issued a confirming order for nearly all patrols. Looking back, I imagine we must have lugged a typewriter up there, unless we found one in the wreckage of the town.

This, of course, was the drill for a set-piece attack, planned and mounted in advance. In fluid fighting, or when new orders had to be given in the midst of action, one would get a wireless message or a signal by runner, and issued one's own orders to the company in the same way. It mattered a great deal in those conditions that the people concerned knew one another and were accustomed to working together.

In our set-piece attack on San Marino, we met nothing worse than accurate machine-gun fire which was extinguished by the tanks. We leapfrogged forward by companies, clearing the new town of what seemed to be a strong rearguard, and by dusk on September 20th D Company were sitting on the very top of the mountain, and the Captain-Regent had accepted the situation; his citizens had helped us vigorously in evicting the Germans. The battalion's casualties were very light, only eighteen wounded. It had been a neat operation which we celebrated with a good dinner in the albergo in the old city, and by turning out the pipes and drums in full fig next day to play for the notabilities of San Marino and for the Army Commander and Mr. Harold Macmillan.

Autumn arrived with a succession of heavy thunderstorms which turned all the tracks into gluey mud. When the sun came out, the noon heat was still delicious but the nights were chilly in the hills, and we began to think about battledress again. I had found the company in good form, but with substantial changes. Bobby Burns was in hospital and Robin was acting as divisional liaison officer, being replaced by Lindsay Gibson. Almost more important was the loss of CSM Owens, worthily promoted to RSM to replace Jock Campbell; luckily in Sgt. White we had a ready-made substitute and the company still functioned well. I was glad to be back. Apart from my feeling of responsibility for C Company's well-being, it was very pleasant to make the round of the platoons and pick up the threads of personal contact again with the men, in addition to the reins of command through the platoon officers. There had been some local leave which cheered everybody up. I asked one NCO how he had enjoyed his forty-eight hours, and he told me how shocked he had been to see a queue outside the town brothel. 'They wis all sorts, French and Indians and us yins. I jist tellt them it was fair disgustin' to see them all lining up like ferm dogs after a bitch in season, and they should be black ashamed.'

'What happened, Corporal?'

'Ach, they began to slink off afore I'd finished tellin' them what they looked like.'

'And what happened then?'

'Ach, there was naebody left in the queue, sir, so I jist gaed in masel'.'

The wearisome Italian rains had set in again, accompanied by strong gales. It was important to get the company under some sort of cover to give a chance to the sodden patrols of drying out after their night's work. We found a few more or less intact houses here and there, in amongst unlifted potato fields and unharvested tomatoes; the inhabitants of the whole area had been driven out by the Germans when they cleared the countryside in front of the Gothic Line. Houses, of course, meant fleas, but dry clothes were worth the irritation. We were lousy, as well, and the louse powder issued to us set one scratching more violently than ever. We could never decide whether the powder itself was the irritant or whether it stimulated the lice to prodigious activity. A palliative was to wear one's vest and shirt inside out on alternate days; at least it made the creatures work for their living.

Pay helped the company's well-being, too. On September 27th the men had their first pay for five weeks, which fortunately coincided with the arrival of some cigarettes —we were gasping for a smoke—and a beer ration. We also had a foretaste of the future with the publication of schemes for demobilization; however distant the prospect, the fact that the Government had got around to planning it was cheering. And we all had a pay rise, and I could look forward to a jump from 28/- to 32/- a day.

We spent a week at Scorticata after the San Marino action, patrolling and planning the next advance on yet another ridge of hills, Reggiano. For this attack we were under command of 7th Brigade and lined up with the Royal Sussex whom we'd last met at close quarters at Cassino. To get to the party we had to cross the Rubicon, which gave the classicists a field day, although we were moving in the opposite direction to Caesar; I cannot remember whether we found a bridge or had to ford it. C Company's first objective was known as Spandau House which enfiladed the approach to the Reggiano ridge and had to be taken before the main advance was launched. There was a great deal of noise from our guns and from the enemy, and strong wind and heavy rain made control difficult—just the conditions in a night attack when a raw unit can come a cropper. But the company went about the business steadily and methodically; after capturing the house we pushed on to Borghi, a village just beyond it, our limit. The Sikhs had been ordered to pass through us and exploit forward, but for some reason were not allowed to move on at once, and had to hang around in our company area. After reporting our positions to battalion and going round the platoons to make sure that they were in shape to beat off any counter-attack, I went back to my HQ, in a farmhouse, bent on getting some sleep; I don't believe I have ever felt so exhausted, my eyeballs were burning in their sockets. The tiny room was filled with chattering Sikhs whom it would have been churlish to kick out, so I lay down amongst them where the company signaller could tug my boot if a message came through, and thankfully passed out.

The company had come off lightly. The battalion's saddest casualty was the death of Willie Cameron of B Company, a fine officer and a most delightful young man whom I had first met when he was a schoolboy. The war seemed to be dragging on and on, we were only three-quarters of the way up Italy and on the western front the Allies were by no means over-running the Germans yet; we had forgotten our cheerful hopes of finishing the thing off by Christmas. There appeared to be no end to attacking one ridge after another, and for the first time I began to think that the only alternative to ending up like dear Willie with a bullet in the head was the good fortune of getting one in the arm or the leg and departing to hospital. Resilience is a prime quality in a soldier, in most occupations for that matter, and by this time my stock of it had run low, though one could not afford to admit it even to oneself. It was with relief that I took the company back on October 3rd when we were ordered out of the line and went into rest, though I wondered sourly for how long and in preparation for what new task.

9

PARTING

WE got back into battledress with a gloomy conviction that another winter campaign lay ahead of us, while tremendous falls of rain reminded us what the Italian winter would be like. I at least had a change of scene, for I was despatched on another round of hospital visits, leaving with Finn in our jeep on October 6th. First call was to see David Douglas, now running a transit camp; lunch, and much talk of things in general and the battalion in particular. Finn and I made poor progress in the afternoon, the roads were so muddy and carrying so much traffic, and we found ourselves miles from anywhere, long after dark. Not the weather for a bivvy, so I pulled in to a large farmhouse and asked for a room. 'So now I'm writing to you,' I told Louise, 'on the kitchen table, surrounded by round-eyed kids, while Papa sits by the fire smoking Players and Mama is locking up the rations she's been presented with. Finn cooked an excellent supper for us, the political and military situation has been well and truly discussed, I have had to tell them all about myself—"Voi che moglie? Ah, bravo, una moglie! E quanti bambini? Non ne ha del bambino?—Ah, la povera!" They have now retired to bed and left us in sole charge of the kitchen, where our two beds are all ready.'

I found seven General Hospitals, though only twenty of our wounded in them, which was nothing like the full tally. Most of the men were coming along pretty well apart from one lad, not much over nineteen, who had lost a leg and had a shattered shoulder, with the other arm broken. As usual, I came away with a long list of letters to be written to relatives. There was no time to track down more hospitals; as it was we covered nearly 1,000 miles in four days, on every one of which it poured with rain. Luckily it eased up in the evening, and we could get the bivvies up, and Finn could cook supper, before it teemed down again. I made only one diversion from the strict path of duty on our way south, a half-hour visit to the church at Loreto, superb in richly intricate detail; I was anxious to see the source of the once-famous shrine at Musselburgh, torn down in the Reformation, which gave its name, mis-spelt, to my school. We had to come back through Rome, where we spent a great evening of talk with the Avolios, in atrocious French since as usual my even worse Italian made them laugh too much to converse; after breakfast next morning Finn and I were seen off by the entire family, promising that we would be back as soon as we could. A final day's furious driving took us back to the battalion's new location, Montepulciano, where they had moved in our absence.

It is an entrancing little hilltop city in the pleasantest part of Tuscany; we were in billets scattered all over it, C Company being very snugly housed in a school. The place had suffered no damage in the fighting, and to walk along streets not piled up with rubble and past buildings with roofs intact and glass in the windows was a refreshment in itself. The usual routine of 'rest' swung into gear; all kit and weapons checked, damaged items repaired or replaced; inoculations for everybody, I've forgotten against what save that it wasn't shellfire; leave parties organized and sent off in batches; a reading and writing room to be fixed up, and a canteen opened; local recreation arranged, which meant football and indenting for a mobile cinema; then a few spit and polish parades to show that we could still put on the dog, and some gentle field training and marching.

I found myself going through the motions without a great deal of enthusiasm. I was bone-tired day in and out, the more so because to the company one could never appear tired. All I wanted to do when I was off duty was to sit in my billet and absorb the beauty of my room. Teddy Cameron, Charlie Cameron, the Doc and I were billetted in the Casa Bracci, where we enjoyed the most agreeable fortnight of our stay in Italy. The Conte Bracci was something of the city magnate in manner and appearance, but the Contessa was every inch the great lady; tall, grey-haired, very handsome and with a charming smile which mitigated her commanding presence. Their house had a severe sixteenth-century façade of the honey-coloured local stone, a refacing of a much older building; within, a fine stone stair led from the hall to suites of rooms which had been refurnished at different periods. The library had been untouched, a glorious room with a fifteenth-century painted ceiling, the alcoves and desks of age-blackened oak and a collection of manuscripts and books to take one's breath away; they and the pictures were in the process of being brought up from the cellars where they had been hidden. The room in which the Contessa put me had white painted walls, black beams making an intricate pattern on the ceiling, faded crimson hangings and carpet, a large oak writing table with silver fittings, four seicento paintings, one of them a very beautiful Assumption. I felt layers of fatigue peeling off like onion skins as I sat in that room, and when I climbed into the four-poster at bedtime between the coronetted sheets — sheets! — I could hardly bear to put the light out and stop looking at it.

I was asked if I would enjoy an evening of music. We sat in the salon listening to gramophone records of Scarlatti and Beethoven, a curious assortment, and to one of the three young Bracci boys playing the piano, very well. The entire battalion was receiving this sort of kindness from the people of Montepulciano and a return was called for, so we mounted a full-scale parade of the pipes and drums in the square, followed by a drinks party for as many as we could cram into the *palazzo municipale*. This was a great success, and led to even more hospitality being showered on us. Since practically all the Jocks had been packed off on leave, the officers were ready to enjoy all the fun that was going. For me that included being shown by the bishop the cathedral's collection of Siennese paintings, still hidden in the crypt, and a day's shooting on the Origo estate among the woods which had recently sheltered dozens of allied prisoners on the run. We knew at the time something of the extraordinary risks the Marchese Origo and his wife had taken in helping escaped prisoners of war under the noses of the Germans, but it was not until I later read Iris Origo's *War in Val d'Orcia* that I realized the full extent of their heroism.

Somewhere I was introduced to a man with a passion for puppets; he was always known as the Engineer Patella and, I suppose, was a retired civil engineer. One thing led to another, and the upshot was a multi-lingual puppet performance of *The Tempest*, in a severely truncated version, the difficulty being to maim the Italian translation in line with the English text. Miranda and Ariel of course were Italian, as was Prospero; Ferdinand and Antonio were Camerons, and so was Caliban. To add to the complications, Trinculo insisted on reading his part in French. It went something like this:

Caliban	As I told thee before, I am subject to a tyrant, a sorcerer, that by his cunning hath cheated me of the island.
Ariel	Tu menti.
Prompter	Pietro—Peter—Calibano!
Caliban	Oh, sorry—er, Thou liest, thou jesting monkey, I do not lie.
Stefano	Trinculo, se interrompi ancora il suo raconto, per questa mano, ti farò saltare via qualche dente.
Trinculo	Certes, je n'ai rien dit!

Rehearsals were a test of Italo-Scottish comity but the performance was a riot. The Braccis let us use their library; we invited the brigadier and the officers of the battalion, and the townsfolk who had been so good to us. The Contessa received in state, the electricity didn't fail, the music was good, the dialogue or rather cross-talk ran well if confusingly and the puppets were wonderfully manipulated by the Engineer. His masterpiece was the storm scene, with effects—lightning, thunder, heaving billows, a tossing ship, tempestuous music—that brought the house down. Afterwards there was tea, the boys put on the gramophone and we all danced. When eventually everybody had gone and I thanked her warmly for her kindness, the Contessa said movingly that we had created an evening of the most light-hearted happiness that she had known for years.

For me, one of the happy touches was having Robin Collier in the party, paying us a visit from divisional HQ. It was particularly good to see him because he had just been awarded his M.C. for the Monte Grillo counter-attack. His visit was a reminder of what a happy company we had been in C for the last two years, and led me to ask myself some questions. I felt tired and stale, but that could be expected to pass off. More serious was the fact that I wasn't hitting it off with Alistair Noble and this, I thought, would have repercussions on the company. Alistair must have had an unenviable task in taking over as the fifth C.O. of the 2nd Camerons, if one counted the two acting commands, in six months, and particularly in following Moggs Hill; and doubtless I had reached a state of bloody-mindedness when I would have gone looking for trouble with the Archangel Gabriel. The outcome was a suggestion by the brigadier that I should put in for a place at the Staff College. I swithered for a week because I was convinced that, if there had to be a war and if one had to be in the army, there was more fun and satisfaction in regimental soldiering than in anything else. And giving up C Company would be a painful wrench because I felt almost proprietorial in my pride in commanding it—a very sound reason for my being replaced, as I came to realize later. In the end I sent in my application, though I doubt if I should have done so had I known that it meant another eighteen months away from home in India and and the Far East.

Immediately afterwards I was whipped off with the C.O. on a three-day trip to Rome, which was good of him. I saw the Avolios again, and jumbled up a Ginger Rogers film, *Coppelia* and the *Barber* with visits to bookshops and the Vatican. Then off by way of Naples to rejoin the battalion which in our absence had moved to Taranto — I had a marvellous run of luck in missing the tedium of battalion moves. The usual crop of rumours about our destination now agreed that we were not going back to the Italian front, and proffered instead various theatres from India or Burma to the Middle East; I don't think even the wiseacres prophesied that the division would be sent to Greece.

Meantime we were back to a round of parades, inspections and guard-mounting which at least made a change from patrols and attacks. The company was cheerful, everybody had enjoyed their leave and nobody was sorry to miss another winter campaign in the north. White was showing himself to be as good a CSM in this relatively peacetime routine as he had been in battle. He was an excellent judge of temperament and timing, which is the key to correct tuning of that many-stringed instrument, an infantry company. Genuine peacetime began to look a possibility in 1945 as far as the war in Europe was concerned, which led to an administrative panic over the terms of engagement written in every soldier's paybook. It was feared that D o W, or Duration of the War, had been entered in some cases, which could be construed as permission to go home after an armistice, whereas the correct D o E, or Duration of the Emergency, was for the authorities a nicely open-ended commitment. I took exception to the order from Army HQ that the paybooks were to be examined without disclosing the reason to the soldiers, and was almost sorry to find that all C Company paybooks, as in the rest of the battalion, carried the correct formula. With a sound preference for the real to the empty abstraction, the Jocks interpreted it as Duration of the Enemy.

Another streak of an impending civvy dawn was the opportunity to register a proxy vote for a future general election. Some of the men needed a little pushing and persuading to take action over this, but we eventually completed the job for the entire company with one exception. This was Corporal Fairfax who I now learned was stated by the civil authorities not to be a British subject. Fairfax took it as a joke and not an insult, but the rest of the company were indignant since he had proved himself a brave and intelligent soldier. Would he have been disowned as the alien son of German-Jewish refugees had he been captured by the Germans and treated by them as a traitor? Battalion and brigade were equally incensed, and his case was taken up vigorously, though I left Italy before I knew the outcome.

If the division had been sent back to north Italy, and if the fighting that winter had proved severe, I am not sure how we would have performed. There had been no sign up to that time of the company's ever being 'sticky' in action, of responding slowly to orders or dragging its feet in the advance (with one possible and partial exception, an officer who thereon departed abruptly). But to go through it all again with a real prospect, and not just a dream, of returning to wife and family and home could possibly have made us all a little over-inclined to keep our head down. Against that is the fact that the battalion proved highly effective in difficult conditions in Greece. Keeping some sort of peace between EDES and ELAS, the right and left wing factions engaged in civil war, called for all the military virtues, and it cost casualties.

What makes a soldier fight? It is after all a highly

unnatural activity, save perhaps for the rare moments of hand to hand, face to face combat when animal rage and a determination to survive at the other man's expense are the driving forces. One has to look for something more cold-blooded to understand what makes a man step out of shelter and move forward in an advance, or sit tight in his slit trench under bombardment, waiting for the enemy attack. It would be uplifting, no doubt, to think that a conviction of the righteousness of his cause was the motive, but I don't believe it. The cause may provide him with a basic reason for putting on, or being put into, uniform, but assuredly it will not make him actively fight for it, except possibly when it becomes a last-ditch affair of protecting family and homeland. I do not recollect ever discussing in the company the justice or necessity of the war, which were taken for granted; if pressed, we would perhaps have mumbled something about not wanting to see British kids in the Hitlerjugend. The fact that they are not is still the war's justification, as I remind myself as I read of each new student sit-in. There was no private or official attempt to dramatize what we were fighting against, or to inculcate hate against the enemy, always regarded rather impersonally as the Eyeties or the Jerries and never as 'fascist beasts'.

There is a theory that alcohol plays a major role in making men fight, but if that be so I never served in the right campaigns. A rum ration was sometimes issued, particularly before a big set-piece attack, but its real purpose was as a substitute for a hot meal. It was usually several hours' march to the forming-up area with a further wait until the whistle blew for the attack, and it simply was not feasible to get cooked food or even a mug of tea to the troops. Rum at least warmed one up, though the tot available was nothing like enough, unfortunately, to launch one forward in stupefied oblivion of danger or to release whatever atavistic instincts may be supposed to lurk in any combatant. Other considerations apart, the theory falls to the ground in the case of an Indian division where the Muslim soldiers, to whom alcohol is forbidden, were every bit as effective as the others. Whatever may once have been the case, one can dismiss drink along with the hope of loot or fear of flogging.

Individual bravery exists all right. It serves as an invaluable example, and is an indispensable quality for the solitary adventurer, but I doubt whether it is sufficiently common to motivate a body of men. Most people are too sensible for heroics. Yet men in a body can indeed be brave, and to my mind the reasons are trust and cohesion.

Trust begins by the individual's knowing what is going on and understanding the reason for the particular operation ahead of him. He must have the feeling that his leaders, both those he can see and those higher up, know their business and make sensible plans; and since trust can never be produced by a public relations exercise, this means that his leaders must indeed be competent. Herein clearly lay one of the differences between the two world wars; in spite of jokes like calling the elegantly-clad officers back in Cairo the Gabardine Swine, I cannot remember any of the rancorous distrust of the staff or the high command that permeates so much of the writing of World War I. At the immediately local level, trust depends on a man's knowing that his commander thinks of him as a person and therefore treats him fairly, and looks after him — food, weapons, clothing — as well as conditions permit.

Cohesion follows as a matter of course, and this is the root of it. Men are inclined to do what their comrades expect them to do or, more accurately, because nobody actually wants to fight, they do what they imagine their comrades expect them to do. Whether this be mutual deception or mutual support, it does the trick. In the good unit — and trust and cohesion both grow from and create a good unit — the assumption is, of course, that actions will be governed by those never-mentioned concepts, duty and honour.

Neither of them, just idiocy, led me to play a game of rugger on a flint-strewn patch of ground on November 16th. When I hobbled off I learned that I was booked for the Staff College at Quetta while the battalion less C Company was to embark for Greece on the 22nd. Now that the moment had come, I was profoundly sorry to be leaving the 2nd Camerons, the more so because I was in charge of a large-scale brigade demonstration which left no proper chance to say goodbye to old and good friends. But I was still with the company, who were to follow on to Greece in a week's time, though in the novel capacity of being their guest for a few days. Finn clucked around, convinced with reason that I couldn't get on properly in India without him; his care for my well-being was resumed, after we were both demobilized in 1946, in the shape of an embarrassing variety of presents to Louise. The company was taken over by Colin Kerr, now recovered from the wound he had received in September. Since it was he who had introduced me to C Company in 1940, there was a great satisfaction in rounding off nearly four and a half years by handing over to him.

On the evening of the 27th, CSM White and the NCOs put on a party, and next morning I said goodbye to the men. Finn walked down to the harbour with me to make sure my baggage was loaded on the ship, and on the dockside I said goodbye to him. So that was that. It was a good company.

INDEX

Rank, style and decorations relate to the period covered by the narrative

INDEX

INDEX

177

INDEX

INDEX

Watson, Cpl., 55

Wavell, Gen. Sir Archibald, G.C.B., G.M.G., M.C., 5, 28, 34, 37, 52, 68, 81

Webster, Pte., 71–3, 77

West Yorks, 2nd, 76

Western Desert Force, 6

White, Sgt., 98, 109, 162, 170, 174

Winton, Sgt., 98, 128, 149

Young, CQMS, 126